Lyn —

Thank you for such
wonderful hospitality!
God bless,

~ Penelope.

WOMEN BY DESIGN

Women by Design

PENELOPE SWITHINBANK

MONARCH
B O O K S

Mill Hill, London NW7 3SA and Grand Rapids, Michigan

First published by Monarch Books in the UK in 2000,
Concorde House, Grenville Place,
Mill Hill, London, NW7 3SA.

Published in the USA by Monarch Books 2001.

Distributed by:
UK: STL, PO Box 300, Kingstown Broadway, Carlisle,
Cumbria CA3 0QS;
USA: Kregel Publications, PO Box 2607
Grand Rapids, Michigan 49501.

ISBN 1 85424 492 2 (UK)
ISBN 0 8254 6000 X (USA)

British Library Cataloguing Data
A catalogue record for this book is available
from the British Library.

Cover illustration:
Roses, or The Artist's Wife in the Garden at Skagen
by Peder Severin Kroyer (1851–1909).
Copyright © The Fine Art Society / Bridgeman Art Library.

Book design and production for the publishers by
Bookprint Creative Services,
P.O. Box 827, BN21 3YJ, England.
Printed in Great Britain.

For my mother,
who has always unselfishly been there when needed,
and in memory of her mother, whom I still miss.
My thanks for their unfailing love, loyalty,
support, prayers and example.

Contents

Acknowledgements

I am grateful to my family and friends for their encouragement and support.

Wendy Brown and Philippa Taylor gave me the initial encouragement to write this book, and believed I could do it.

Carolyn Armitage and Max Sinclair have been very helpful and always encouraging.

My husband, my daughter Harriet, Pam Stocker and Sarah Rednall read the typed pages and made very helpful suggestions and criticisms.

The members of the Tuesday Bible study group – Anne, Carol, Cathy, Francie, Julia, Janet, Lesley, Pamela, Philippa and Sarah – have been uncomplaining guinea-pigs as we worked through some of the material, and they have kindly allowed me to quote them. They have supported me with their prayers through the difficult times.

Eleanor Mumford has been used by God many times in my life over the past twenty-five years; I owe her so much.

My family – Kim, Robin, Harriet and Victoria – have barely complained when supper hasn't happened because I've been shut in my study; and they have always supported me with their love and prayers.

The dog, Oliver, has insisted I take him for a walk every day. It has been very inspiring!

Thank you.

Introduction

The large bottle of aspirin was still sitting on the top shelf of the kitchen cupboard; I checked it regularly. Bought a few days before, it was my safety net – if I couldn't pluck up the courage to jump in front of a bus, I could swallow some little white tablets. Only I wasn't sure how many were needed to make a desperate plea for help but not actually die.

I opened the cupboard door to check again and my hand crept up towards the bottle. At that moment I hated myself for having got to this stage; I hated my body; I hated my life; I hated the house where we lived and the city it was in. I hated our church and I hated the God who had brought us there to be on its staff.

Something seemed to prevent me from grasping the bottle. I shut the door and turned away, and as I did so I decided to turn my back on God. I blamed him for everything that had gone wrong in my life.

Was *this* what God intended when he designed me?

* * *

For our first Christmas my husband gave me a cookery book entitled *The Pauper's Cookbook* to tide us over the first few lean months. (I'm still using it but that's another story.) It had a recipe for meatloaf which looked good, but the ingredients included two cloves of garlic. I had never used garlic before so I was relieved to discover that there were indeed two pieces of garlic in the box. But when I started to peel the garlic, I was amazed to find lots of little bits inside. It did cross my mind that maybe those were the cloves; but no, the packet had two things in it and if that was the way they came, the recipe was probably right. I was far too impatient to check: my cooking was usually fine and this would be all right too.

That meatloaf had about forty cloves of garlic in it, and for several days afterwards the pupils in my classes remarked on the smell! Had I found out what the instructions really meant I could have saved myself (and my poor husband) considerable embarrassment.

The recipe was clear, but I didn't bother to take a few minutes to understand it. I thought I knew best and could get by.

God had a specific plan in mind when he designed each one of us, and a purpose for our lives. But often we neglect his instructions and the results can be chaotic. God made me a woman, and he made me 'me'. Sometimes I struggle against one or the other, and sometimes I struggle against both. There are times when I want to do or to be things which God doesn't have in mind for me, and that puts me into conflict with him. Conflict can be tiring and emotionally exhausting. My bottle of aspirin was bought at a time when I was feeling very depressed and drained of all energy, physically, mentally and spiritually. I was rebelling against God. He had called us to work in London and I didn't want to be there, and instead of looking to him for strength and support in a difficult situation, I developed a negative mindset. That made me critical and unhappy, and dissatisfied with everything including myself. I have been learning that understanding the design which God has for each of us frees us from negativity, and opens up exciting possibilities and challenging opportunities. It gives us the potential to make a difference for God in the lives of others, in our jobs and in our homes as we allow him to equip us to be all that he intends us to be.

We live in great times for women. We have more freedom than ever before and in theory we can choose to do almost anything we want. It appears that to be a woman now is to be noble and strong, mistress of your domain, whereas a man is portrayed as slightly dim, a helpless inferior being. We are told that three out of four women succeed in business, but only one in five men. Women can 'have it all', successfully combining career and family life. There is the excitement of knowing we can do anything, go anywhere.

But for many, maybe most of us, it isn't like that. Seventy per cent of the world's poor are women, and two-thirds of all illiterate people are female. We struggle and are confused with new pressures, difficult choices, misapprehension. More than ever we need to go back to God's recipe for us as women and as individuals, and then we will be able to begin to achieve all that God intended for us. A woman who is following the maker's instructions and actively pursuing a walk with him will discover a relationship which is life changing and empowering. She is an attractive person with purpose to her life, despite the ups and downs, the successes and failures, the good times and the not so good.

Taking the time to find out what God's purpose is and what he says is challenging. Everyone wants to change something about themselves. We can change our physical appearance to some extent, we can work on our behaviour, but only God can change us from the inside out. Taking time to follow his recipe correctly makes a significant difference.

I hope this book will help you to begin to read God's recipe for you. The ingredients include knowing what we are aiming at; where we can channel our energies; who our role models are, and what we are living for. Only you can choose whether you want to get to know God's plans better, to grow to be the woman he means you to be. Then you will be able to help others on their journey too. Someone once said, 'We teach what we know, but we reproduce what we are.' My prayer is that through this book you will better understand God's design for you and become the woman he intended you to be.

1
Designed by God

For it was you who formed my inward parts; you knit me together in my mother's womb. I praise you, for I am fearfully and wonderfully made . . . In your book were written all the days that were formed for me, when none of them as yet existed. (Psalm 139:13–14, 16)

Jo's house is a bombsite. There are piles of things everywhere; there are things not in piles everywhere else. She has four pretty little girls who rush around at full flight, often in their nightwear, shrieking, laughing, playing, arguing and fighting, all at the top of their lungs. Jo moves serenely among it all, the fifth baby still a large protrusion as I write. Whenever you visit Jo you will be welcomed in, although you'll have to clear a chair before you can sit down, and you'll be persuaded to stay to a meal which magically stretches to accommodate everyone's appetites no matter how many other waifs and strays are also there. Jo is always surrounded by people; they adore her and find her easy to talk to. She's slim and petite and blonde, and very unthreatening. Jo's hopelessly disorganised, of course, and as she keeps neither a shopping list nor a diary there is often chaos. When she has tried to start a list it has invariably got lost and turned up weeks later under a pile of other things, and by then is so out of date it's useless. But there is rarely a crisis in Jo's household; when the untoward happens, Jo can usually laugh or turn it into a funny situation. Jo sometimes worries that her household is chaotic, and wishes she could be more like her friend Paula who seems to accomplish so much each day because she is efficient and well organised.

Paula's home is immaculate; it is polished and tidied and always looks glorious, with a beautiful arrangement of flowers on the old oak table in the front hall. Her three children are neat and clean and 'well presented', as her grandmother would have said – in her day babies were never seen in baby-gros but were always in pristine white gowns. Paula has lists; she is motivated and systematic. If you want a job done Paula will do it and do it well and ensure it is done on time. When you are invited for a meal it is a gourmet's delight, served on time with love and care and attention and you are made to feel really special. Turn up unannounced and you will have disrupted her timetable. Tall, dark-haired and well built, Paula is caring and wants people to confide in her but they often seem rather wary. Yet she longs to be liked and needed, and envies Jo who always has lots of friends and appears to be carefree. Paula feels she never has enough time to do everything that needs to be done; her list of jobs looks daunting and she worries that she won't do things well.

It's no accident

God has different templates for Jo and for Paula, and another one for you. 'For we are what he has made us, created in Christ Jesus for good works, which God prepared beforehand to be our way of life' (Ephesians 2:10). He has designed each person and made each of us unique. He did it intentionally. What a thrilling thought – he made us who we are and there's no one else quite like us! And then we look in the mirror, or at someone else's enviable figure, and we feel somewhat disgruntled. Dissatisfaction sets in.

Rooting out the problem

Maybe, I thought, if I could change my hair colour I'd be happier. So I became a 'suicide blonde' – dyed by my own hand. It didn't suit me! Maybe if I drove a convertible car I'd be more content. So we bought a second-hand one advertised in the local paper. It turned out to have been stolen, and caused us several headaches and hours of sorting out the problem – time which could have been better spent without wasting emotional energies. Perhaps if I changed career right now I'd have more 'quality time' and less dissatisfaction with life. So I taught business studies in a sixth-form college and was miserable; I hadn't thought to ask God where he wanted me. If only, we say to ourselves, I could just be thinner, more organised, better at talking to people, if only I could be different!

Dissatisfaction, with ourselves or our surroundings, with what we are or what we have, causes us to rebel against what God has designed. We try to take control and manipulate things in ways God never intended. Instead of dealing with the root cause of my problem, I often try to find a way to cope with it. It's like weeding – pull off only the leaves and the roots will continue to grow, sometimes even more strongly. Dig down, cut out the roots, and the problem plant is destroyed. Of course, it takes longer and is more of an effort, but the results are long term.

Designed but flawed

Recently our church family had a weekend away together, and on the Saturday evening played various party games. One involved photographs of well-known members of the congregation, seen as children, and we had to guess which was who! One particularly ancient black-and-white photo showed a toddler in its cot with a large old-fashioned tin of Nivea cream which the child had smeared liberally across its face like shaving foam. People looking at the photo immediately saw the likeness between the child and my son Robin, and assumed the child was my husband. But in fact the creamy-faced child was me! I'd taken the Nivea from the chest at the foot of the cot. My son can be seen to resemble both of us: there is a definite family likeness, which all our three children bear. They are very different, but each is visibly our child.

In the same way, each of us bears the image of our heavenly Father, who created each one of us in his own image (Genesis 1:27). God's statement emphasises that both man and woman were created to be like him, equal in importance, equally bearing God's image, made to reflect his glory. Tell yourself that when you look in the mirror first thing in the morning.

As a result of the fall we become hostile to God and dissatisfied. In spite of God's image being stamped on us we rebel. 'I can will what is right, but I cannot do it. For I do not do the good I want, but the evil that I do not want is what I do' (Romans 7:19). We have to learn to hate the sin in ourselves just as God does. With God's help we can fight it, making a daily decision to want what God wants, to choose to follow his plans not our own.

Designed and female

'But I always wanted to be a boy, didn't you?' asked Kathy as we discussed this, and Julia agreed. Some of us climbed trees, read boys' adventure stories and dreamed of living life without the frustrations of being a girl. Others of us were thrilled to dress up as princesses, cradle our dolls and play at tea-parties, delighting in our party frocks and reading stories of girls having midnight feasts in their dormitories.

God made us as women, and it was no accident. That's what he intended for you and me, with all the attendant joys, excitements, challenges and problems. Whether you were a tomboy or a princess, he made YOU the way you are, because he wants you, he loves you, with your determined walk, or your shy smile, your short fingers or your large ears, your blonde curls or your grey layers, your easy-going approach to life or your ability to organise and get things done.

God designed us to be women because nothing else and nobody else could do what we can do! Adam was wandering around in the garden, pottering among his plants, but he was lonely and couldn't manage by himself. Sounds familiar, you think! God brought all the animals to Adam, who named them, but none of them was able to become his partner and equal and work along-side him to help him look after creation. Adam was alone and needed a mate, so God very lovingly created someone who would meet his needs by being his partner and helper, his companion and friend (Genesis 2:18–23). Then God told both of them that together they were to rule over creation and look after it (Genesis 1:26–31). Only a woman could fulfil what was needed when man couldn't do everything by himself and was lonely. (But she couldn't manage alone, either, and got into trouble when she took things into her own hands!)

God designed us as women because we are needed and important. We can be used by God to do much for him and he longs to mould us into women of integrity and influence who reflect God's love and light, who are content to know that God designed us to be who we are. We may be determined, great achievers, strong-minded and capable, impetuous and flamboyant or quiet, shy, cautious and timid. We may be well educated or creative, work long hours, be full-time mothers or live alone. But we can all be God's women, making our lives count for him and having a powerful impact on the lives of those around us as we influence them for God.

Dissatisfaction with being female will cause us to rebel against God's design. Being women of God's design can be liberating and challenging because it is the pinnacle of God's creative genius: he meant us to be female.

Designed and formed

Every year, for a week or two at the beginning of summer, hundreds of women lose an average of five pounds in weight before going on holiday. They suddenly decide that in order to enjoy it, they need to resemble a stick of celery, because that is the shape of the eight or nine top models. We think that life would be better if we could just lose those extra pounds – or cover up the grey hairs, or get rid of the wrinkles appearing at the corners of our eyes. If we're honest, we often dress and diet in order to compare ourselves favourably with other women or to impress other women. Barbara Bush, wife of former President George Bush, is reputed to have said that she thought she was popular because she was old, large and white haired and therefore didn't threaten anyone. The rest of us perhaps long to be young, thin and blonde, and feel threatened by those who are. Thinking along those lines nudges its way into our subconscious because of what we see and hear portrayed as the perfect woman by the media. We feel dissatisfied with ourselves and our bodies. 'Why do I have such horrid legs? Why can't I look like her? Why is my life like this? Why am I me?'

It relieves us of an enormous amount of pressure to realise that we *don't* have to look like someone else or behave like them or achieve in the same way they do. Learning to accept God's pattern and working within it can lead to greater contentment, a greater sense of satisfaction. The Lord 'made you [and] formed you in the womb' (Isaiah 44:2). In other words, he intended you to be the way you are. None of us should look at ourselves and feel second rate. We can choose instead to look at ourselves as God does. Of course, he hasn't finished working on us inwardly yet. He wants to mould us, just as a potter shapes the clay into the pot or bowl he has in mind. Isaiah says that God is the potter and we are the clay, the work of his hand (Isaiah 64:8). The clay can't say, 'Why have you made me like this?' (Romans 9:20). Sometimes the potter has to squash the clay together and start again if it has gone wrong. God is able to do that and remould us into the shape he originally intended, as Jeremiah described (Jeremiah 18:4). Our physical looks may not change much, but our character can be radically changed by God, which may well alter our facial expression and appearance as his light shines through us.

Gladys Aylward grew up despairing of her black hair and her 4'10" height. Her friends at school were tall and elegant, and had pretty hair, blonde or red or brown. As a young woman, she heard God's call to go to China to work for him. When she arrived she looked at the people around her and exclaimed, 'Lord, you knew what you were doing!' The Chinese were short and dark haired, and Gladys realised she would not be conspicuous or an object of wonder. She would fit in and be able to work alongside them. God knew what he was doing when he designed Gladys.

There are those who are good with people and those who are good at tasks; some are flexible and available while others work to time and get things done efficiently. Some are tall and others short, blonde or dark, or . . . just like you. 'For we are what he has made us' (Ephesians 2:10). Accepting how God has designed us gives freedom to concentrate on the more important things he has in mind for us.

Whose am I?

Mary has helped me by her example. She was a young girl about to be married, probably both joyful and fearful, keeping herself pure for her wedding night, when she had the most dramatic and frightening experience: an angel stood in front of her. His opening words say much about her: 'Greetings, you who are highly favoured! The Lord is with you' (Luke 1:28, NIV). She must have had a close relationship with God to be described in such glowing terms. Of course she was worried and alarmed, especially when he went on to announce that she was to have God's Son as her baby before she was even married. Yet there was no hesitation, no doubting or refusing. She didn't bewail the loss of her own plans or wonder if it would make her happy; she didn't argue that she was too short or not pretty enough; nor ask for time to think about it or even pray it over. She was curious as to how it would happen (well, who wouldn't be?) but her tone must have been very different to that used by Zechariah, her cousin's husband, when the same angel told him that he and his wife would have a baby. Zechariah doubted and disbelieved and Gabriel imposed dumbness as a punishment. Mary's genuine curiosity as to how God would act was gently answered: 'The Holy Spirit will come upon you.' Her immediate reaction was total obedience, whatever the consequences. She might be misunderstood by Joseph and her family and friends; people would talk; but she didn't hesitate to be used in whatever way God required of her. She was content to leave it to God: 'I am the Lord's servant.' OK, God, whatever you say. This was complete surrender, at whatever cost, to God's design.

What did Mary tell her family and friends – and did they believe her story of angels and God's baby? Or did they sneer, consider her cheap, doubt her word? I think Mary was a woman of integrity, and her quiet trust in God would not have gone unnoticed over the years. Yet it must have been hard in particular for her to face her parents. God had designed Mary for something special. Clearly she put God first in her life and trusted him even when it was tough. She knew life would be difficult and was warned when the baby was small that 'a sword will pierce your own heart'. She watched her first-born son die in utter agony and disgrace. But she remained with the disciples afterwards, still trusting God and his design for her life.

Isobel Kuhn, when called by God to go overseas, faced a mother who had prayed for missionary work for years. She had been president of the Women's Missionary Society and held missionary prayer meetings in her home. Yet she said, 'Over my dead body!' when Isobel told her of God's calling.

God had a design for Isobel and she knew that anything else would be second best. There was no thought of being unable to go to foreign lands because she was a woman, or because she didn't have the 'right' looks or the 'right' temperament. Isobel obeyed God and went. She never saw her mother after she left for Bible school. Her mother died following an operation, but the night before she died, she said she knew Isobel had chosen the better part in devoting her life to the Lord. Later, Isobel received a letter from her mother's friend, telling of her mother's change of heart. It was a blessing on the calling. The way had not been painless but 'God first' was her life motto: full and glad surrender at any cost.

God formed us in the womb (Psalm 139:13) and we can praise him because we are so wonderfully made (Psalm 139:14). He knew what we would be like before we existed (Psalm 139:16). There is great security and contentment in knowing we are meant to be the way we are. We belong to him and he loves us, in spite of, or perhaps because of, the way we are put together. We can pull ourselves up to our full height, smile at ourselves in the mirror, and know that 'we are what he has made us, created in Christ Jesus for good works, which God prepared beforehand to be our way of life' (Ephesians 2:10). Having designed us he calls us to what he's prepared us to do.

Putting it into practice

At the end of every section you will find some thoughts and questions to help you think about what you have read and to encourage you in your own spiritual journey. You might like to work through these on your own, with a prayer partner, or with another woman you are helping and encouraging in her walk with God. Sometimes it's good to jot down thoughts and ideas to use as prayer items or to look back at later and see how God has been at work in you.

• Spend some time thanking God for the way he has made you – for making you YOU.

• Meditate on Mary's story (Luke 1:26–56). Ask God to speak to you.

• What does Mary's example show you in your situation?

• Is there anything about yourself which you find hard to accept? Ask God to deal with that, and for the power of his Spirit to help you see yourself as God sees you.

• Thank God for aspects you like about yourself; concentrate on these, and gradually add to your list as he shows you new things.

2

Designed for a Purpose

No eye has seen, no ear has heard, no mind has conceived what God has prepared for those who love him. (I Corinthians 2:9, NIV)

It was late afternoon in January and I was on the slopes of a snow-covered mountain in Austria. Soon it would be dark. Because there had not been as much snow as usual, the lower part of the ski runs were patchy and difficult; large boulders emerged from thin snow, and icy patches were numerous. As a tentative skier, I was terrified, stuck on the mountain and unable to get down. The chair-lifts were still working but the man on duty at the top had refused to let me ride down. With me were two men, both competent skiers, one being my husband. They tried to stay by my side to encourage me down but it worked best when my husband went in front and showed me where to go. He tested it first and then I followed, step by step as it were, ski by ski.

We twisted and turned, and all the time I trusted my guide I was able to move. But then I took my eyes off him and looked at the whole panorama in front of me, and the long way still to go. I panicked; I was completely unable to move. So I sat down, removed my skis and said I would walk – I love walking, normally. My guides pleaded with me to put the skis on again and warned me I wouldn't be able to get down the mountainside in boots. But my nerve had gone completely, and I sat in the snow, terrified and shaking with fear. I have to confess they summoned the 'piste-basher' machine to fetch me; and I have not skied since.

I was surviving when I followed the one in front and went where he went and tried to copy him; I failed when I tried to do it my way and looked too far ahead instead of concentrating on the next step.

Follow my leader

Jesus described himself as the good shepherd, with his sheep following him. That may sound strange to Western ears, because we are used to seeing sheep rounded up, often by dogs who chase them into line. But in the East, the shepherd leads his flock; he knows each of them by name, and when he calls they follow him. He goes first to find a safe route and look for good pastures. The sheep trust him and recognise his voice. That is the picture Jesus had in mind: he is ahead, finding the right paths for us and we are to follow where he leads us, knowing that we can trust his choice.

Just like my skiing escapade, there is safety when we fix our eyes on the one in front, when we have a leader who knows the best and safest way to go. Jesus is a leader who has been there before us, lived a human life. My skiing companions could not understand – they were fearless on skis, and considered my fears irrational. Jesus is different; he can empathise with us, knowing and understanding just how we feel. He will lead us through life when we listen to his voice and respond to his call.

Chosen for a purpose

Premeditated

God 'created [us] in Christ Jesus for good works which God prepared beforehand to be our way of life' (Ephesians 2:10). In other words, he made us the way we are because he chose us specially, knowing what our futures would be. The future belongs to God and he's worked it all out ready for us. 'Before I formed you in the womb, I knew you,' God told Jeremiah (Jeremiah 1:5) and Isaiah said that the Lord had called him before birth (Isaiah 49:1). Both of them knew that God had called them to be prophets. The Old Testament tells the story of a people chosen by God. The glorious choosing continues in the New Testament for us. 'In him we were also chosen . . . according to the plan of him who works out everything in conformity with the purpose of his will . . . for the praise of his glory' (Ephesians 1:11–12, NIV). God has a purpose for each one of us, determined even before we were born. He knows what he is doing: he thought it all out beforehand. Isn't it exciting to think that he has such wonderful things planned for each of us, plans formed of old, faithful and sure (Isaiah 25:1, RSV). God chose me, God chose you. We're special.

Promised

After God chose people in the Old Testament, he often gave them a sign to show that he meant it. Samuel anointed David, the son of Jesse, who had been chosen by God to be the next king of Israel (1 Samuel 16:1, NIV), and then the Spirit of the Lord filled David powerfully as a seal on the choosing. Having been chosen (Ephesians 1:11), we too are given 'a seal, the promised Holy Spirit, who is a deposit guaranteeing our inheritance' (Ephesians 1:13, NIV). God has chosen us, and gives us his Holy Spirit as a pledge to confirm his choice.

Called for a purpose

'It would be much easier to cope today if I knew what was going to happen in the future, or even next week!' Often, when talking with friends about God's purposes for us, we desire to know the whole of God's plan, as if it would be easier to cope with the day-to-day details if we knew what the next ten or twenty or thirty years were to be. But I'm not sure that it would be very helpful to know everything God has in mind for us. Some of it *will* be wonderful and enjoyable, but there will also be times when he has to discipline and test us or our loved ones and that may well be painful. There will be joys and sadnesses, encouragements and disappointments, celebrations and mournings. Life will go up and down. How wise God is to shield us from too much knowledge. *He* knows, and he is to be trusted. 'For surely I know the plans I have for you, says the Lord, plans for your welfare and not for harm, to give you a future with hope' (Jeremiah 29:11). We don't have to worry about the future – most of what I worry about never happens or at least not in the way I feared. 'I trust in you, O Lord . . . my times are in your hand' (Psalm 31:14–15).

Standing at the crossroads

When God calls he doesn't force us to go his way. We are free to choose. 'He is silently planning for thee in love' is an old translation of Zephaniah 3:17. He knows which way is best for us, but we have a choice and each decision we make is like a crossroads where we decide which road to take. Even if we make a wrong decision and take a step outside his plan, he can work things out if we ask him and allow him to take charge. 'We know that all things work together for good for those who love God, who are called according to his purpose' (Romans 8:28). If we truly love him then we will want him to guide and direct because we trust him to have our best interests at heart. When we set off down the wrong pathway we're telling God he's wrong. But if we stop and confess he'll lead us back on to his way again.

Answering the call

I've been inspired by the example of women who have responded to God. One in particular has helped me as I read her books. Amy Carmichael heard God calling her to be a missionary and ten months later she began training with the China Inland Mission. She'd packed her trunk ready to sail, but the door to China was closed when the doctors refused to pass her as medically fit. It was the first rejection of several, but she knew God had called her and that he would lead her in the right direction in his own time. In fact it was nearly three years later that she finally arrived in India. Other missionaries said Amy Carmichael would not last six months as she arrived so ill and weak. God planned otherwise. He had called and he knew where he wanted her. Amy spent the next fifty-five years, without a furlough, running a home for needy children, many of whom she rescued from temple prostitution. The last twenty years of her life were spent confined to her bed at Dohnavur. She still had work to do for God, both in providing a home for the needy children who became her adopted family and in her writing, most of which was done during the bedridden years. Her published letters and thoughts have given spiritual guidance and insight to many over the years.

God had a purpose for Amy's life and she waited for him to show it to her and then she faithfully stuck to his plans for her in spite of opposition, illness and lack of money. She achieved a huge amount in southern India, although she hated to be in the limelight and tried to refuse the honour bestowed in the Birthday Honours List. Yet when she first responded to his call to 'Go!' she had no idea of where she was to go or what she would be doing. Could any of us cope with knowing all that God has planned for us? One step at a time is probably enough for most of us.

Equipped for a purpose

I asked my daughter to help me in the kitchen. I needed a good selection of cakes and biscuits ready in the cupboard – her siblings were coming home for the holidays. Having asked her to make a cake, I then made sure that she had everything she needed to do the baking. She started the task with the right ingredients. Having begun cooking, she soon got into the swing of it and decided to make a couple of her favourite tray bakes as well. She knew that would be appreciated. But the margarine ran out, so I gave her the money to go and get some more. I was equipping her with what she needed for the task.

When God has chosen us for a purpose, he calls us and then equips us with everything we need to do that job for him. He doesn't leave us to struggle on by ourselves. He gives what is needed to 'equip the saints for the work of ministry' (Ephesians 4:12).

Equipped to prevail

After David was anointed and filled with the Spirit, he attacked Goliath, the enemy of God's people. He did it in God's strength, discarding the large heavy suit of armour and using only the simple sling and stone which he used in the fields. He was a young, untrained shepherd boy but he prevailed against the huge

Philistine. He went out in the name of the Lord, and he told every-one 'the battle is the Lord's' (1 Samuel 17:47). God has vast resources available to help us, whatever our particular battle. When the circumstances are tough, when we feel unable to do what he's asked us to do, when we feel depressed, he has more than sufficient to meet the need. He equips us to prevail.

My Bible has red underlining on many pages where I've noted the verses which have helped me at particular times. These verses are often promises of God, or descriptions of his love and power and strength. Paul said that Scripture will equip us for every good work (2 Timothy 3:16–17) and I've proved that – even though I do forget and have to be reminded! Reading those verses again, and hearing God's voice speak to me through them, can be very pow-erful. 'Penelope,' he says to me, 'you can do all things through me because I strengthen you; nothing is impossible for me; I do not grow tired or weary; I give you grace to help in times of need; I am your strength and your song; I am your arm every morning; I give power to the faint and I will increase your strength; I will strengthen your weak hands and make firm your feeble knees; I will uphold you with my victorious right hand. He will keep me going to the end because he 'is faithful and he will do it' (1 Thessalonians 5:24, NIV). Knowing that this is my God, I need have no fear in attempting great things for him within his wonder-ful plan for me. He turns my weaknesses into opportunities for his strength and power to be seen at work, and then the glory is his.

Equipped to be protected

David was chosen, called and filled. He prevailed against one enemy, but 'Saul remained his enemy for the rest of his days' (1 Samuel 18:29, NIV). Several times, David feared for his life when pursued by Saul, but God always protected him. David could say that God was his refuge and fortress. He delivered him and pro-tected him (Psalm 91:2, 4). David was living close to God. We can know the same protection because nothing can separate us from the love of God. We can be 'more than conquerors through him who loved us' (Romans 8:37, NIV).

God is our shepherd: 'Jehovah-raah' who looks after his sheep.

Sometimes he needs to pick us up in his arms, or rescue us from rocky precipices, or fend off wild animals. He is the good shepherd, and we shall never be snatched out of his hand (John 10:28).

God is our shield: A shield in Old Testament times was a large, cumbersome, wrap-around affair, leaving only the soldier's back unprotected. As long as he advanced behind his shield he was protected. Only if he turned and ran was he vulnerable. God's shield for me is his plan for my life – nothing can get through that unless I'm in retreat from his plans.

God gives us his Spirit: When I accepted a proposal of marriage, I was given an engagement ring as a pledge of the fullness of love to come. In the same way, we have the Spirit of God within us as a pledge, or 'first instalment' (2 Corinthians 1:22). The Spirit gives us inward protection, and teaches us to become dead to sin (Romans 6:11). A dead person does not respond to any stimuli, however loud or violent. That's how the Spirit wants us to be – impervious to the stimulus of sin. He changes us from the inside out. It takes a lifetime for him to do it and there will be times when we fail, but God's Spirit never gives up on his protection as he works in us.

Finding God's purpose

Following the right paths

How do I know God's purpose for me? How do I find out where I should live or what job I should do? Who I should help and influence? Whether to go to university, and if so where? Whether or whom I should marry? God knows best, but how do I find out?

LISTEN to God's voice

What if I can't hear God's voice telling me which way to go, what decision to make? Sometimes it feels as if it would be easier if God shouted to tell me his purpose. But his voice is often the still small voice after the noise of the wind, earthquake and fire, as Elijah discovered (1 Kings 19:9–13). Learning to recognise God's voice, learning to hear it, takes time, and sometimes we don't make time to listen. The winds of doubt and indecision; the earthquakes of feelings and desires; the fires of busyness and wrong priorities – these can cause us to be deaf to God's voice and open only to other voices in our lives. We have to take time to listen.

FOLLOW God's footsteps

Sometimes he shows us his footsteps so we can follow, or he shows us the path clearly set out in Scripture. At other times, it isn't until we look back at a period in our lives that we realise how God has led us safely through various circumstances or made sure that we followed a particular path. Often the timely shaping of events with the confirmation of Scripture verses have together pointed us to the right decision.

No overtaking

I am often in a hurry, tearing around to get things done. When I'm driving, I hate being caught behind a slow-moving tractor or caravan and do my best to overtake so that I can go at my own speed. I like to be in front, in charge of how fast I'm going, and can get very impatient if I have to wait. When I am following God and waiting for him to lead and guide me, I can get very frustrated. Instead of waiting for the sense of peace that comes when I follow him, I want a definite signpost so that I can charge ahead. But God isn't in a hurry, and I have had to learn that it isn't wise to overtake him.

Map reading

Sometimes it's hard to know whether a plan is our own idea or God's. We get excited about something, we feel we've got the vision and we want to go full steam ahead. How do we test whether it's God's purpose for us?

Take your ideas to God. ('Commit your work to the Lord and your plans will be established', Proverbs 16:3.)

Test your ideas against the principles in the Bible. ('All one's ways may be pure in one's own eyes but the Lord weighs the spirit', Proverbs 16:2.)

Trust God and his wisdom. ('Trust in the Lord with all your heart, and do not rely on your own insight', Proverbs 3:5.)

Put God first in all you do. ('In all your ways acknowledge him and he will make straight your paths', Proverbs 3:6.)

Keep abiding in him. ('Take delight in the Lord, and he will give you the desires of your heart', Psalm 37:4.)

Ask wise Christian friends for their prayers and advice. ('Fools think their own way is right, but the wise listen to advice', Proverbs 12:15.)

Check if it will help you in your walk with God. ('You ought to live and to please God more and more', 1 Thessalonians 4:1.)

Make sure it isn't a stumbling block to others in their walk with God. ('Resolve . . . never to put a stumbling block or hindrance in the way of another', Romans 14:13.)

Echo the prayer of Jesus: 'Not my will but yours.'

And a final question: Why am I doing this and whose approval am I wanting? If you're doing it because it's God's purpose for your life and you want his approval, go ahead and follow where he leads.

God's purposes in action

Ruth was a strong-minded young woman who had suffered pain and loss but who chose to submit to God's design for her and then saw his provision in every situation. It actually all began with a married couple, Elimelech and Naomi, who took their two sons and left the unrest and famine of their own land of Judah and went to live in Moab, a country condemned by God. After that, things went seriously wrong – first Elimelech died, then the boys married Moabite women but then the boys also died. Had it been a joint decision by Elimelech and Naomi to leave their home and go to a strange country? Did they stop and consult God? The fact that everything went wrong would seem to suggest that they went outside God's plans and took things into their own hands. But God was still sovereign and was still at work.

Eventually, Naomi heard that things were better at home, so she set off with her two daughters-in-law. Along the way, Naomi suggested that the girls stay in their own land as she could no longer provide 'rest in the home of a husband' for them. Orpah, whose name means stubbornness, actually gave in quite easily, but Ruth, whose name means friendship, was tenacious and insisted on accompanying Naomi. Here was a young woman who was prepared to give up her own homeland to go to a strange country and take on all the customs and religion of the new land. Her lovely, steadfast promises are often used in the context of love and marriage, but she spoke them to Naomi. No room here for mother-in-law jokes. 'Don't urge me to leave you,' she said. 'Where you go, I will go . . . your people will be my people and your God my God. Where you die I will die, and there I will be buried' (Ruth 1:16–17, NIV).

Ruth stood by her promises. She was determined to go, and she went. She had made the decision to follow Naomi's God and all the rest fell into place and was used by God in his sovereign plan.

The women of Bethlehem welcomed Naomi home, but she asked them not to call her Naomi, which means pleasant and sweet, but to call her Mara, which is bitter. She didn't know whether to blame God for all that had happened or to acknowledge that he was in control. After all, it wasn't God who had told them to go to Moab. It must have been hurtful to Ruth to hear Naomi say to the women that she'd returned 'empty with misfortune'. Even if it was, Ruth bore no malice, nor did she put on airs and graces and say, 'Look what I'm doing for my mother-in-law.' Instead she offered to go out to work to support them both. Life for two women would have been difficult in those days without a man to look after them. So Ruth went to 'glean': gathering the grain left behind by the workers in the field. 'And as it happened . . .' (Ruth 2:3) – what an understatement – 'she came to the part of the field belonging to Boaz, who was of the family of Elimelech.' Co-incidence or divine appointment? God had planned that Ruth just happened to walk into the right field at the right time, a field belonging to Boaz, Naomi's relation. God provided food and protection as Boaz gave orders that she was to have extra food left in her way and she was not to be molested by the men. Ruth's reaction was modest: 'Why me, a foreigner?' even when Boaz told her that people were praising her for what she was doing for Naomi. He prayed that God would reward her richly;

and as sometimes happens God answered the prayer through the one who prayed it.

When Ruth got home, she told Naomi everything. Naomi immediately thanked God that he had not forgotten them and had not stopped showing his favour. Naomi began scheming to 'find rest in a home' for Ruth. I love that little phrase for wives – rest, or security, in the home of a husband. That is where the contentment of a wife should be. Ruth, however, didn't set out to look for happiness, an ephemeral feeling at the best of times, nor was she specifically looking for a husband. She was wanting to ensure that they were looked after and she obeyed Naomi without question, knowing that Naomi's God was faithful. Yet Ruth was no shrinking violet, judging by her earlier behaviour and statements. She risked everything, her reputation and therefore her home and livelihood, to obey. God blesses those who obey.

What Naomi now suggested was Eastern custom: claiming the protection of a relative for a young widow. She told Ruth to lie at Boaz's feet while he slept guarding the grain. To approach a man from the foot of the bed was a symbol of submission and humility. Naomi also told Ruth to make herself attractive with perfume and her prettiest dress: no harm in looking one's best for these things. So Ruth obediently uncovered his feet and lay down. Everything was done according to the laws God had given to Moses and the nation of Israel.

Did Ruth fall in love? She certainly listened and obeyed. She trusted God – even when Boaz said there was another man who might have a prior claim. Imagine being disposed of like that! But Ruth waited patiently, and her faithfulness led to great joy. The other relative didn't want to marry Ruth so Boaz took her as his wife. Their friends prayed that the home and family would be blessed by God, and God's answer proved to be far greater than they would ever have guessed.

It was part of God's redemptive plan. Ruth's son was the grandfather of King David, and from David the genealogy goes all the way to Jesus. God knew. All that time before, he had it planned.

Ruth shared her joy by letting Naomi care for the boy. The women said that Ruth was better than seven sons for Naomi (Ruth 4:15). She had come under the wings of the Almighty for refuge (Ruth 2:12). Her obedience and trust, in allowing God to guide and direct her life, led to contentment for her and great blessing for everyone.

Obeying God's purposes

Chrissie is a high-jumper and competes in athletics events around the country. She often has to jump when there are other field events going on around her and she has learnt to fix her eyes on a stationary point in the distance which is higher than the bar she is to jump, and aim at that. She knows not to glance at any other movement around her. 'I concentrate on that one thing and leap towards it,' she says. 'Yes, it is hard, and I'm tempted to think that other competitors have an easier task if they are just running or sprinting. But I know from talking with them that each event has its own particular difficulties. All of us take part to win, though!'

Like those athletic events, we each have our own race. Although other people's hurdles or obstacles may not look as difficult as our own, it's no good comparing. We each have to concentrate on our race, fixing our eyes on a stationary point for which we aim. 'Let us lay aside every weight and the sin that clings so closely, and let us run with perseverance the race that is set before us, looking to Jesus' (Hebrews 12:1–2). We 'keep our eyes fixed on Jesus' (GNB) and follow him, knowing that the reward awaits us at the end – to be with him for eternity.

Putting it into practice

• In what ways have you seen God guiding and directing your life? Spend some time thanking God for the way he has guided you.

• Share your experience of God's guidance with a friend. Encourage one another as you see God's faithfulness in each other's lives.

• Meditate on Ruth's story (Ruth 1–4). As God speaks to you, ask him to guide you in his purposes for your life.

• Can you trust God for future guidance? How do you know?

3

Broken Designs

Christ Jesus came into the world to save sinners – of whom I am the foremost. (1 Timothy 1:15)

The water was running down the wall of the kitchen, dirty rusty-coloured water. It dripped onto the work surface and spread into the line of cookery books; it splashed down onto the side of the dog's basket and created a puddle on the blue blanket. It formed a river on the floor and crept towards the door and the hall carpet. Half way up the wall, the boiler was emitting volcanic eruptions and deep-throated gurgles as water gushed from it. I had only been out for a short while, but it hadn't taken long for what seemed to be a torrent of water to wreak havoc in the kitchen and to make the dog extremely upset.

A phone call to the diocesan plumber, followed by his prompt visit, led to the discovery of a crack in the boiler. It was an old model and overheating had caused it to give way under the strain. However, a new boiler would be expensive, and so the crack was mended and we hoped for a few more years of hot water and heating. But old, warped, leaky boilers are not very reliable. Eventually, it gave out, there was another leak and the plumber admitted defeat. A new slim-line boiler was installed in the basement. It is very quiet and extremely effective, and supplies constant hot water and wonderful heating, even in our enormous house.

The mess left by the old boiler took a while to clear up but today there's nothing to show that there was even a kitchen in that room, let alone a boiler or flood. It's now my study: the same room with the same dimensions, doors and windows, but utterly changed.

A faulty boiler or a leaky cistern are worse than useless: they are unreliable and make a lot of mess. Most of us would opt for the new model every time. It seems obvious. Yet faced with the choice of a fountain of fresh clean water, or a leaky cistern, some people chose the latter. 'For my people have committed two evils: they have forsaken me, the fountain of living water, and dug out cisterns for themselves, cracked cisterns that can hold no water' (Jeremiah 2:13). The comparison is clear: God is the fountain supplying living water, freshly available, never running dry. But instead of taking this wonderful water which is offered to them, the people preferred to try out other ways of satisfying their thirst.

Digging our own cisterns

Well, of course, I would never do that, would I? Dig my own leaky cistern. And yet, if I'm honest, how often have I turned away from God, tried digging my own cisterns, and discovered they leak? Instead of looking to God as the fountain of life I've looked for satisfaction from elsewhere. Instead of acknowledging that God has a plan and purpose for my life, something for which he has designed me, I've chosen my own way. Sometimes I've tried to dig a really big cistern, sometimes just a little one. Not one has given lasting satisfaction: each has let the fountain of life ebb away. What happens when we break the design and purpose God chooses for us?

We lived nearly four years in London. My husband was on the staff of a large West End church which provided us with a tall Victorian family home in Highbury. It was, in many ways, a lovely house, with plenty of space, and we were able to decorate it and make it our home. But I hated it. The garden was minute, hemmed in by high walls, and every window in the house looked out at other houses. After living in a beautiful Somerset valley, walking the dog by the river and canal every day, watching the colours of spring and summer and autumn, I felt desolate. The church was full of lovely people, but there were so many of them that I found it hard to get to know anyone, and not being an extrovert, I didn't make any extra effort. Instead of going to the fountain of life to be refreshed each day and be given the grace and strength I desperately needed, I tried other things instead.

I was running my own business, and I threw myself completely into that, giving it all my attention and energy. I was trying to find satisfaction, and did, to a certain extent. But I blamed God for taking me to London, for having to leave friends, and the dog. I blamed him for the hour's school run twice a day, the half-an-hour's tube journey to church each Sunday with the children, as my husband went earlier with the car. So I gradually cut myself off from the fountain of living water, and dug new cisterns for myself. I worked hard, nothing wrong with that, but I did it to shut God out and leave no space for him. I spent any spare time reading; nothing wrong with reading, but what I read was not always wisely chosen and I used it as an escape from the pressures of life, work and family.

My values began to change: I wanted more money in order to have a 'better' lifestyle, expensive clothes, continental holidays, theatre tickets, dinner parties. None of these things were inherently wrong; but my attitude to them was. I was seeking satisfaction and happiness from them, and I was tempted away from the true source of life and satisfaction. I could blame it on God, I could blame it on my circumstances or my upbringing, or on the influences of the media and the world around me. It was the eighties, and I was niche-marketing maternity wear for businesswomen and hiring out ball gowns and cocktail dresses. I conformed to this world because I hoped it would quench my thirst. It didn't. I therefore decided that the only solution was to move back to Bath where I had been so happy and where I presumed I would find contentment again. I had no thought of what God might want, just a determination to pursue my own way and dig my own cistern.

Discovering the leaks

I moved Bumpsadaisy, my maternity wear business which I had
started from scratch and now franchised to over seventy people,
back to Bath. My dear husband, who had been considering itinerant ministry for some time, was offered a new job which allowed
him to work from home, and subsequently we bought the house
of my dreams. It took a year to 'do it up', complete with limed-
oak kitchen with Aga, en-suite bathrooms and designer wallpa-
pers. Yet never had we been so unhappy. My husband realised
that his heart was in parish work after all, the business was
having problems, we were overstretched financially, and the
stress told on our marriage. There came the day when we told
each other over the phone that each was on the brink of leaving.
We were both horrified at what we had said, and it served to bring
us to an abrupt halt. A year after moving into that house, we lost
everything as the recession hit and we suffered as did many
others. On the surface, I was successful: two homes and a time-
share, a nanny, three cars (one for her), children in private education, and all the rest. But underneath was a leaky cistern, and it
leaked in a big way. We ended up with our furniture in store,
owning absolutely nothing and moving with just our clothes to
live with my parents-in-law. Everything I had based my life on
had gone and I was left empty.

So who's in control?

'Don't you just love to be in control?' asks a television advertise-
ment, and it's true, we do. So much so that we are frightened to be
seen to be out of control in any sphere of life. I wanted to be in
control, to be seen to be capable and successful, able to manage
everything – my home, my emotions, my children, my work. I
must be seen to be able to go it alone and achieve everything for
myself, handle the difficult situation, the imperfect relationship,
the balance of work plus home plus relaxation. I couldn't
acknowledge, even to myself, that I felt inadequate; and I couldn't
admit my need or be seen to be dependent on anyone.

Familiar feelings, some or all of these. They come from the old sin of pride. I was too proud to admit my fears. Too proud to want others to see I'm not perfect. Too proud to acknowledge my need of God and let him take control, to give him myself.

Excuses for not returning to the fountain

What prevents us returning to the fountain of life? For me, it was mostly pride, but also a desire to conform to what was going on in the world around me, and envy of what I saw some of my friends were able to afford. Had I verbalised my feelings, this is what I might have said:

I'll lose control of my life

Physically I always feel this when faced with a downhill slope, even if I'm not on skis. A wet, slippery slope is a nightmare, but even on a dry, sunny day I dislike going down hill, terrified that I will not be able to control my steps and fall. Outwardly, I think I succeeded in fooling most of the people most of the time. I worked hard at the office; I ran a clean, tidy, efficient house; my children were polite and well dressed; the cupboard was full of home baking. No one saw the control needed to send the children out of the way to enable me to be busy, busy, busy. When friends came to stay, there wasn't a ready-made meal from a certain superior supermarket in sight. Actually, I'm surprised they still came.

But behind the efficient facade was a lonely person who had for-saken God and who knew the gap that left. I had little or no time left for relationships, with God, my family or friends. I shouted and screamed at my husband and my children in my effort to control them. I needed to learn to let God take over the reins of my life. He had to teach me the hard way: I didn't learn easily. So the business collapsed and with it went the material possessions and the public image of the successful woman. I was out of control in a big way. It was terrifying. I had thought I was secure. God had to bring me to a place where I could say, 'Lord, I can't run my own life, never mind the universe. I give control to you.' 'Trust in the Lord . . . Take delight in the Lord, and he will give you the desires of your heart

. . . Commit your way to the Lord; trust in him, and he will act'
(Psalm 37: 3–5).

I feel under pressure to conform

The world is tempting. 'Upward mobility' was the cry of the eighties and early nineties. Everything had to be bigger and better than
anyone else's, everyone had the right to what they wanted, and
credit was freely available. I fell for it, and lost my contentment,
along with much else.

'Anything goes,' the world cries at the turn of the century.
Freedom and tolerance: believe what you like, take a little religion
from here and a little from there. It's so easy to be influenced by
the world's way of thinking, even if we try hard not to be. We are
subtly duped into thinking that this or that is all right, is indeed an
inherent right, just because it is becoming part of what is accepted
by those around us or those who dictate to us through the media.
We are all influenced by our culture, our education, our traditions,
the media, the general climate of our age, whether we like it or not,
whether we think we are or not.

What pressures do you find hard to resist? Is it to move in with
your boyfriend? To move away from your husband? To declare
your sexuality as being different? To work longer and longer at the
office in the quest for more prestige, more money? To have an
abortion? To have the latest fashion accessory, the most exotic
holiday, the thinnest fittest body, the satellite dish, cable television,
or less easily defined things, such as the right to self-justification.
They are each things which the world says are right and necessary
but each can tempt us away from God.

The pressure of those we mix with most of the time can be very
strong and it is not easy to stand firm and alone. When my children said, 'But everybody else does!' I replied, 'If everyone
jumped off a cliff, would you jump too?' To which one daughter
replied, 'Depends what's underneath!' But the other said, yes, she
would jump because she wouldn't want to be left behind if all her
friends had jumped. That desire to be part of the crowd and be
accepted is very strong; and can lead us into doing or being what
is not part of God's design. 'Jesus Christ . . . gave himself for our

sins to set us free from the present evil age, according to the will of our God and Father' (Galatians 1:4).

I'll have nothing left

An addiction, or a way of life, can be like a comfort blanket. We rely on it for security and strength. It gives an escape route from the pressure and stress of everyday life. Maybe it's a secret 'vice' that we keep hidden from others and into which we retreat when things get too much to cope with. I used two things as my retreat: voracious reading of any book I could get my hand on, and often it was a trashy blockbuster; and alcohol – a stiff brandy as soon as I got home from work, a glass of wine, or several, with my evening meal. I was using them to escape the real issues I should have been facing, and I began to rely on them.

We can come to rely on all kinds of things. Drugs, which include stimulants like coffee and tea, as well as sleeping pills, tranquillisers, or even aspirins and laxatives; bingeing, even if it's just on chocolate biscuits; alcohol, the sherry or glass of wine without which you can't get through the evening. Or the sexy or racy book, video, television, sport, cigarettes. Even the need to be accepted, the desire to be seen to be successful, the worry about what others think of us. If they were removed we fear there would be nothing to shore us up, nowhere to hide, nothing to comfort us. They are chains which bind us. We make resolutions to break the addictions, but resolutions themselves seem to be made to be broken. Life-controlling habits are not easily discarded however small. But with God's help they can be broken.

I had to learn the hard way. The way of life I had dug for myself didn't satisfy, and in the end I lost it all. Looking back, I am sure that God had to let my business fail before I was prepared to hear his voice again. It was painful but now I am glad. 'He has showered down upon us the richness of his grace – for how well he understands us and knows what is best for us at all times' (Ephesians 1:8, *The Living Bible*).

I'll do it gradually

Hanging on to even one tiny little thing, tucking it away and sometimes not even acknowledging that we're hanging on to it, means that complete restoration can't happen. I kept thinking, 'When God has got me out of this mess – if there is a God – then I can begin to work this out.' We argue with ourselves, 'I can't be expected to change all at once . . . It's too painful, too costly at the moment, I can't cope with sudden change . . . I'll cut down gradually to avoid withdrawal symptoms.'

Paul recommends being drastic: 'Kill everything in you that belongs only to the earthly life' (Colossians 3:5, *Jerusalem Bible*). Be ruthless, cut it out, put it to death. Only when the conscious decision to stop or let go has been taken can the healing process begin. Only then can God begin to deal with the underlying root cause. Can we trust God to heal us? 'He heals the brokenhearted, and binds up their wounds' (Psalm 147:3).

I'll be all alone

One of the things I dreaded most about losing my business and a certain lifestyle was that my friends would no longer like me and would look down on me. My friends aren't shallow or worldly people; it was just that I had an irrational fear about it. In fact, the opposite proved to be true – good friends stuck by us, and now we know some of them more closely than we did before. But I worried that I might be left penniless and friendless.

Most of us need people. Few of us could be like Julian of Norwich, who lived in the fourteenth century, alone in a tiny cell attached to the back of a church. Without interruptions and distractions she was able to spend her time in solitude so that she could pray, meditate and reflect on God. She received long visions from him, which she later wrote down, about the divine love. Julian learned to live alone with God – for those of us with busy, noisy lives this sounds like bliss. Yet for most of us it would be difficult to live without understanding family and friends around us. We may fear losing them if we choose God, especially if some of those closest to us don't know and love God themselves.

I realised that I was dependent on another human being when I heard Max Sinclair preaching about heaven – no, I wasn't dependent on Max, nor on the preaching. He described how Jesus will be all that we need, for everything. There will be no need for other people because we will be totally caught up with worshipping the Lamb of God; and although we will all be worshipping together, we will not *need* the others around us and certainly will not have a special relationship with any one of them. It was as if I had been physically punched in the stomach, and the tears started to my eyes. I *need* my husband. He is my friend, my companion, my lover; my children's father and my constant support. He makes the difficult phone calls, helps me to survive criticism, is patient when there's too much month left at the end of my money. He laughs at my annual joke and puts up with my foibles; he warms my feet in winter and takes the splinters out of my finger. Supposing I had a problem in heaven. Who would sort it, or me, out? And for a fleeting, awful moment, the thought crossed my mind that I'd rather not go to heaven if I didn't have my husband beside me. It was quickly followed by the irreverent thought that not to go wouldn't help because he'd still be in heaven even if I wasn't, so that didn't solve the dilemma! I'm glad I love my husband, but do I love Jesus more? Is he all that I need?

Is there a relationship or friendship that it would be hard to give up? That would leave you alone? Is there someone I love, depend upon, more than Jesus? God isn't asking that we turn away from relationships. He gives us all things richly to enjoy (1 Timothy 6:17), including human love. But do we love him *more* than anyone else? Is he the first and most important person or relationship? Is our love for him so great that our love for others is almost like hate in comparison (Luke 14:26)? God promises to keep us company. He can be trusted to be the 'true friend [who] sticks closer than one's nearest kin' (Proverbs 18:24). He can be a husband (Isaiah 54:5). He is our refuge and strength (Psalm 46:1), a rock, fortress and deliverer (Psalm 18:2).

'Whom have I in heaven but you? And there is nothing on earth that I desire other than you' (Psalm 73:25).

It will cost me too much

'My flesh and my heart may fail, but God is the strength of my heart and my portion forever' (Psalm 73:26). Relinquishment is painful. It's as if your heart will break. God can mend a broken heart, but you have to give him all the pieces, even the bits you want to hold on to or hide from him.

A pencilled note in the margin of my Bible says, '"I turn with disgust from everything to Christ," F.W.R.' Whether it was something I read or someone I heard speaking, I don't now recall, but it's a powerful image of the contrast between what the world offers and what Jesus supplies. When I was a student, I heard a very moving story about a young couple who had recently married and set up home. It wasn't a very luxurious home by today's standards, but it was their first home together and they loved it. So they wrote this prayer together: 'O God, who has given to us so richly of this world's goods to enjoy, help us to live so lightly to them and so wholly to you, that were they all removed tomorrow we should scarcely notice the difference.' Can we say that of our possessions?

On my fridge door, I have a little magnetic card which says, 'If Jesus Christ be God and died for me, then no sacrifice can be too great for me to make for him.' That quote, which I find I need to read regularly, was written in the nineteenth century by a young man from a privileged and wealthy background, who went to Cambridge where he did well academically and was famed for his cricketing skills. He gave up a promising career, the possibility of playing cricket for England, and a family fortune, in order to be a missionary and serve God in China, India and then Africa.

Sacrifice isn't a very popular concept at the moment, when the prevailing fashion is 'me first' and 'what's in it for me?' A sacrifice is a passionate, total self-giving and yielding up of everything. It's a response to the abundant, steadfast love of the Lord which never ceases (Lamentations 3:22) and who gave up everything for me. Sacrifice knows no limits because it is the offering of absolutely everything, without asking for anything in return. Jesus saw a widow putting some money into the collection at church, and he knew that she was giving her last coins to God (Mark 12:41–44). She had nothing left, but she trusted God to provide materially. Can we trust God that much?

Once, when she was very small, my daughter grabbed a tiny

bead in her hand and clenched her fist tightly over it, refusing to let go. I had to prise her fingers open, which hurt her, but I knew the small bead could harm her if she swallowed it. Eventually the bead was released.

God sometimes has to prise our fingers open when we try to cling on to something we regard as precious, but which to him is very small. We hold on in our pride and greed, forgetting that God wants to pour down blessings on us if we would only let go of that comparatively insignificant thing. If we hold out an open hand, giving to him all we want to hold on to, he can and will bless us by pouring down priceless pearls of great beauty to replace the little plastic bead we think so important. Can we trust God?

'My God will fully satisfy every need of yours according to his riches in glory in Christ Jesus' (Philippians 4:19).

The fountain of living water

The God who reveals himself

After the business collapsed, I decided that God did not exist and that my life was a sham. I did the right things and said the right things; I could play the part of a clergy wife, but I did so unwillingly and ungraciously. Outwardly I was conforming to people's expectations as we moved to a new parish and I helped my husband to start in his new job. But inwardly I was bruised after all I had been through, and in some ways it was like a bereavement. Then one day an invitation arrived to a conference for clergy wives. I liked the cartoon on the front of the form, and I knew one or two of those who were organising it, and my husband suggested I might enjoy a few days away in the peace of the countryside. So I went.

On the second afternoon, a guest speaker arrived to give a talk on being a clergy wife. She gave a good talk – biblical, practical, funny. But then at the end, she said, 'Now let's stand to pray and ask the Holy Spirit to come and minister to us.' My fleeting thought was, 'Oh, no, I don't want this, it's not part of my type of Christianity!' However, I stood as instructed, and as I did so, I was suddenly overcome by the presence of God. I knew, without a shadow of doubt, that God existed and was there in that room with us. I saw a bright light flash quickly across in front of me, and a warmth surrounded me and wrapped around me. I was absolutely amazed but at the same time I knew that this was God and he felt right and good and special. The speaker was going round praying for different people but I didn't want her to come near me then. I wanted to be alone with God. She told me later that she knew she shouldn't pray for me at that moment. (She has done so many times since, for which I am profoundly thankful.)

I went to my room, opened my Bible and there was John 4, the story of Jesus meeting a woman at the well in Samaria. I read about a woman who, like me, had been trying to dig her own leaky cistern to find satisfaction, but without success – she still needed to find the water of life which gives fulfilment. Jesus offered her water which would be a 'spring of water gushing up to eternal life' (John 4:14). Again, I experienced something I had heard about but never known for myself: the words were alive, standing out from the page, reaching deep into me. It was a very special time as God spoke to me, graciously revealing himself to me as the fountain of living water. I came home a totally different person from the one who had turned her back on God. My husband wasn't quite sure how to cope with a wife who was suddenly close to God after all the time of doubt and coldness! God is kind and loving as he draws us back to himself. I know others had been praying for me to find God again, and he answered their prayers. He will do the same for you if you want him to.

The God who forgives

Just a few weeks later, weeks when I had spent hours studying God's word, speaking to him and learning to draw close to him again, I woke up one Saturday morning feeling depressed and weighed down. The heaviness deepened during the weekend, and by Sunday night I felt as if I was in the bottom of a well of darkness and despair. Then the tears began to flow and great sobs wracked my body as God began to deal with the time ten years before in London when I had made that conscious decision to turn away from him, tempted by the bottle of aspirin to make a cry for help when everything in my life had gone wrong. There needed to be an acknowledgement that I had behaved wrongly towards God and towards others; I had hurt him, my family and myself. I had to admit my attitude and my actions had been wrong, something I had not previously wanted to admit.

Then I had to say that I was sorry, to my heavenly Father and to my husband who had suffered through my actions, and ask for forgiveness. Immediately, the love and mercy of God came flooding in, cleansing and restoring, lifting the oppression of sin and setting me free. The sense of relief and of release from that burden I had been carrying was enormous. I wrote in my journal, 'I experienced a calmness and peace and sense of forgiveness.' Since then, when I have been tempted to shoulder the guilt and the burden of all that again, God's Spirit has enabled me to remember that he has given me complete cleansing and forgiveness.

God redeems us so that we are renewed like an eagle (Psalm 103:5). We were made to soar like eagles, not to sit in the cage of sin. Jesus opened the door to my cage when he took over my sin for me. The sin is taken away once and for all. It's taken as far as the east is from the west (Psalm 103:12).

The scribes and the Pharisees brought to Jesus a woman who had been caught in the act of adultery. They were wanting him to condemn her and to commit her to being stoned to death, which was the legal punishment for such a crime. Leviticus 20:10 said that both the man and the woman should be stoned. It was a trap set for Jesus. He refused to fall into it and suggested that any of them who were without sin should throw the first stone. They melted away, knowing they were unable to meet his criterion, and the woman was left alone facing Jesus. In his love and mercy and compassion, he did not condemn her, because he loved her as she was, but he did tell her to 'Go your way, and from now on do not sin again' (John 8:11). He condemns the sin, but he loves the sinner who repents. She went out faced with a choice which would result in an action for the future. We too have a choice. God forgives, but it is a subtle tactic of the enemy to keep us looking back and forgetting that God has both forgiven and forgotten. 'He delivered me, because he delighted in me' (Psalm 18:19) – just as I am. God, make me what you want me to be so that you can delight in your handiwork.

The God who satisfies

The story in John 4 that I read on that clergy wives' conference was about a woman who had a large leak in her cistern: she had completely broken the commands of God and was living a rather disreputable life. It didn't satisfy her, and she felt as if she was thirsty for something else. She moved from man to man to try to find one who would fill the gap, but without success.

One day, as she went to get some water, she met a foreigner who asked her for a drink. Bemused, she wondered aloud why he was asking her, a despised foreigner, and he turned her words around and suggested that she should ask him for water because he could give her living water. 'But, Sir, the well is deep and you haven't got a bucket. How can you possibly get water?' she asked. And when he said that he could get hold of water which, once tasted, meant the drinker would never thirst again, she begged to try it. She didn't want to be thirsty ever again. He really had her attention now, and told her to go and fetch her husband. She said she didn't have one; and immediately he pointed out a home truth: 'You're right; you've had five husbands and the one you're living with at the moment is not your husband!'

Her quest for satisfaction had taken her through several men, but none had lasted. The world had not satisfied. Only Jesus could give her the living water which refreshes and satisfies. He wanted to give it to her, but first he had to deal with the sin in her life. She did try to sidetrack him, and got more than she bargained for!

I discovered that only Jesus could satisfy my deepest longings, when God met with me. He showed me the large cracks in the cistern I had tried to dig for myself. When I began to seek him in my daily life, reading his word, talking to him and listening to him, he did what he said he would do: 'But whoever takes a drink of the water that I will give . . . shall never, no never, be thirsty any more. But the water that I will give . . . shall become a spring of water welling up, flowing, bubbling, continually . . . to eternal life'

(John 4:14, *Amplified New Testament*). The period of renewing and refreshing was very special.

But it hasn't always stayed that way. In the few years since, there have been many ups and downs as I have wandered away from God and been tempted by 'the world' again. I have to learn to acknowledge daily my dryness and thirstiness and ask God to refresh me. 'As a deer longs for flowing streams, so my soul longs for you, O God. My soul thirsts for God, for the living God' (Psalm 42:1–2). Our needs can never exhaust God's supply because it is a limitless supply of grace. Are you thirsty? Are you in a dry place at the moment? God will minister the living water of his Spirit to those who ask: lift your hands and receive from him.

Putting it into practice

• There is nothing which is too difficult for God to mend and forgive. You may feel very broken, and know that you have dug your own leaky cistern, and therefore stepped outside his design for you. But God longs to welcome you back. Read and meditate on Psalm 51, which was written from the depths of David's heart after he had tried to find satisfaction in the arms of a married woman. After confession, read Luke 15:11–24 and allow God the Father to welcome you back with his loving arms wide open to hug you. This whole experience may take time: ask God to be at work in you by the power of his Holy Spirit to renew and restore you.

• Maybe one or two of the excuses for not returning to the fountain of living water resonated with you. Ask a friend to pray for you and with you over this. Ask her to keep you accountable once you have decided on the course of action you might take to relinquish your leaky cistern.

• If you have a friend who is digging her own cistern, start praying for her to come back to the fountain of living water.

4

Designed for Relationship

When you search for me, you will find me; if you seek me with all your heart. (Jeremiah 29:13)

Sunday lunchtime, and as usual the meal was late. Our three toddlers were cross and tired and hungry. The youngest couldn't last any longer. Her head drooped into the bowl of food which was in front of her on the high-chair tray, and she fell fast asleep. We laughed, and found the camera, poor baby, and so she is immortalised in the family photo album head down in the food. Then her father picked her up and bore her away to her cot for a proper sleep. So a precedent was set: every Sunday lunchtime he took her for her nap and they began to enjoy this special time together. On many occasions she climbed onto his lap as soon as she had finished eating; and as she didn't eat much she was often there long before anyone else had emptied their plates. She is now a teenager, and is still to be found sitting on her father's lap at the end of the meal, enjoying their special relationship together.

Can this help us to imagine our own relationship with God our heavenly Father? Is this a picture of how he welcomes us to snuggle up to him? If we have not had approachable fathers who mirrored the heavenly Father's attitude, this can cause problems in our relationship with God. My own father was a dear man, and his heart was in the right place; but he was authoritarian, extremely strict, and strongly believed that to spare the rod was to spoil the child. The rod therefore was not spared! I think neither of us found it easy to be demonstrative. He must have been hurt by my independent spirit and my desire to go my own way. Our relationship was not perfect, and it coloured my relationship with my heavenly Father, whom I then saw as a person to be feared because of his authority over me, his displeasure at my wrong doings, and his discipline in my life. My communication with God was formal, even cold, conducted along the correct lines but without emotion playing any part whatsoever.

If it has been like that for me, how much more difficult must it be for those women whose fathers have been unloving or even cruel. Sadly, there are some fathers who are tormentors and meddlers, who undermine and belittle their daughters. There are women who have never known their fathers. Some women have only seen a series of different men in and out of the house and their mother's bed. Other women have been told that, because God is male, they will not be able to relate to him at all. And yet this God, who designed us and who has such wonderful plans for us, wants a living relationship with each of us – because he loves us.

God my Father

I have come to know my heavenly Father much better over the past few years. I still don't know him as well as some people do, nor as well as he would like. But I have learnt to know him more intimately than ever before, and this has happened in two ways. There has been the gracious work of the Holy Spirit in my life, and this has led to my spending more time with God. It's really a sort of 'chicken and egg' situation – the one leads to the other. The more time I spend with God, reading the Bible and praying, the more the Spirit is able to work in me. The more the Spirit is at work, the more I want to spend time with God. 'For all who are led by the Spirit of God are children of God. For you did not receive a spirit of slavery to fall back into fear, but you received a spirit of adoption. When we cry, "Abba! Father!" it is that very Spirit bearing witness with our spirit that we are children of God, and if children, then heirs, heirs of God and joint heirs with Christ' (Romans 8: 14–17).

'Abba' is the Aramaic word for Father, or even Daddy; and that's what we can cry out to God our Father. It's the everyday, intimate cry of a small child and it points to a very special relationship with a loving and caring Father. We were created for a relationship with God and until we begin to know him, there is a void in our lives. 'Thou hast made us for thyself and our hearts are restless till they find their rest in thee,' St Augustine wrote beautifully centuries ago. If that's the way we are intended to function, then it's no wonder that we have problems when we try to find other things to fill the void.

How can we become more intimate with God and be open to the Spirit working in our lives? I have found that it helps to put myself physically where the Spirit can get through to me. That might be at a Sunday church service, or at a Christian conference; it might be while I'm reading the Bible or a Christian book or listening to a Christian tape of teaching or worship music. It might be on a walk in beautiful countryside when I determine to concentrate on God, and sometimes, when there's no one around, I pray and sing aloud! I know that I don't give the Spirit much opportunity if, for instance, I'm constantly glued to the television, or I never read a Christian book or listen to a Christian tape.

To find out more about my heavenly Father, I took my Bible and a notebook, and used a concordance to look up every verse which mentioned God as Father. It took me hours, over many days, but it was worth it. Not only did I learn much, I also enjoyed every single minute as the riches of God began to open up to me and I immersed myself in reading about him.

An everlasting Father

There are some things in life which seem as if they will never end – usually things we are not enjoying and want to end quickly. The things we really love often pass all too soon. It can be difficult to imagine something wonderful which goes on for ever. One of God's titles is the 'Everlasting Father' (Isaiah 9:6). He will *always* be our Father, whatever happens. His promises never fail and can always be trusted. No matter what we do, how far we try to get from him, he is still our Father, and he wants us to approach him. If God seems far away, who has moved? Certainly not God.

A knowing Father

We have a large garden, with a vast expanse of grass. Fortunately the man of the household is responsible for cutting it, and he gallantly walks miles pushing the lawnmower up and down. Sometimes when he is very busy or tired, he asks our teenage son to do it for him. Robin is never asked to mow the lawn in June or July because he suffers from dreadful hay fever and it would be agony for him to do it then. His father knows him and knows what he can and can't do and doesn't even ask in high summer. Our heavenly Father has 'compassion' on us, just as an earthly father does, because 'He knows how we were made; he remembers that we are dust' (Psalm 103:14). Or, as the old RSV translation says, 'Thou knowest me right well' (Psalm 139:14). God our Father knows us through and through. While this may make us feel ashamed at some of the things he knows about us, it is also a great relief. In spite of what he knows about us, he still loves us utterly and completely.

A generous Father

Beth's father gave her a new sports car for her twenty-first birthday; Laura's father gave her a lavish wedding celebration; Jane's father gave his daughter a lasting memory of happy times as they enjoyed art galleries together; and Kate's father passed on his musical abilities to her. But none of those fathers gave anything like as generously as our heavenly Father gives to us. There is no end to his giving. Think of some of the things he has given to you already – he has 'lavished' his love on you (1 John 3:1, NIV); he gave his only Son to die for you (Romans 5:8); he has crowned you with his steadfast love (Psalm 103:4); adopted you as his child (Ephesians 1:5) and poured his love into your heart by the Holy Spirit (Romans 5:5). And he longs to give you more: 'If you then, who are evil, know how to give good gifts to your children, how much more will your Father in heaven give good things to those who ask him!' (Matthew 7:11). Don't be afraid to ask: your loving, generous, heavenly Father is longing to hear from you and wants you to ask him for the good things he has in store for you.

A Father to the fatherless

Some American churches have a 'buddy ministry' for children who, for whatever reason, have only one parent; they are linked within their church to a Christian adult who can be a special 'buddy' or friend to them. The adult cannot replace the absent parent, but helps the child to learn to relate to another adult and to do some of the things they would otherwise miss. One of the special roles God has is that of 'father to the fatherless' (Psalm 68:5, NIV). He is also the helper of the fatherless (Psalm 10:14, NIV) and he wants us to call him Father and not turn away from him (Jeremiah 3:19). Does that resonate with you? God can be much more than we ever dreamed possible. This is a wonderful promise for us all, but especially for those whose image of a father is less than perfect: God is an extra special Father.

God fills and overflows anywhere where we have a gap in our relationships. He is a husband to the widow (Isaiah 54:5), and some single women, whether unmarried or widowed, have found great comfort in addressing him as such. He comforts us like a mother (Isaiah 66:13) and there are many who have found a refuge in his warm, loving embrace. For those whose fatherly image is broken or empty, or full of hurt and bitterness, the complete picture of God is as father, mother, husband, who gives unconditional love, support, help and encouragement; who never fails us, never leaves us, never stops loving us.

A loving Father

'Tell me about God's fatherly love for you,' I urged my women's Bible study group. And they told me; they talked of a Father God who is not limited in any way, who is the greatest and best, whose love is protective and ambitious, and who gives teddy-bear hugs. He never disappoints, he never departs, and his love is perfect. Then we had to find verses in Scripture to back up those claims – and we did, all except for the teddy-bear hugs! But that was how it seemed to feel to be loved by God, and we did find verses that talked of our closeness to him and of his loving arms embracing us (eg, Isaiah 40:11). Nothing can separate us from this amazing love (Romans 8:38–39), which is completely trustworthy (Psalm 52:8), steadfast (Psalm 117:2) and abundant (Jonah 4:2).

'Steadfast' is a glorious word. It means constant and unchanging, and it comes from two other words, 'stead' meaning to establish and fix (like the old homestead), and 'fast' meaning not to be moved or shaken (like making a boat fast or secure). 'Abundant' is plentiful, overflowing, more than enough. What richness we have in God's love! He made the world to show his love (Psalm 119:64). What's more, God wants to prove his love for us, so he sent his only Son to die for us (Romans 5:8).

God's love has redeemed us (Isaiah 63:9) and keeps us safe (Psalm 40:11). It is everlasting (Jeremiah 31:3) and it is lavished upon us (1 John 3:1). But it is also a demanding love. God wants to make us perfect so that we can share his holiness, and so he disciplines those whom he loves. God loves us so much that he wants us to be like him and even though discipline may seem painful at the time, it is worth it because 'later it yields the peaceful fruit of righteousness' (Hebrews 12:11).

God's love is complete. I knew that in my head and I sang about it and told others about it. But I didn't know it in my heart and I didn't experience it. One day in a prayer time, Francie had a picture for me from God. Now, she didn't know anything about my background or my feelings for God, but she had a strong sense of God telling her about this little girl wearing a red raincoat and playing by herself on a see-saw. God said he wanted to come and play on the see-saw too and he sat on the other end so that they could balance and bounce and have fun together, as so many fathers and daughters do. As this scenario was described to me, I was filled with an overwhelming sense of God's fatherly love for me, and a deep desire to know more about it and to experience it in my life each day. The see-saw was the only thing in the playground that I enjoyed when I was a child, but I often couldn't find anyone to sit on the other end, and a see-saw is not much fun on your own.

Several months later when I had forgotten all about that see-saw, Davina was praying for me and she shared an image that came into her mind of God dancing with me. He and I were having great fun together; and I was wearing a red frock. Now I confess I have nothing red in my wardrobe – I was brought up to believe that nice girls don't wear red. This picture from God was of breaking out from tradition and enjoying life with him. I have yet to make a red purchase, but a friend to whom I told all this presented me with a pair of red socks as a start!

God wants to show his love for you and for me; he wants to have fun and enjoy things with us. Sometimes there may have to be times of discipline or times of trial, but there are also times of laughter and happiness. God is a Father whose company we can enjoy. He is fun to be with. Have you experienced that for yourself? You could try telling him that you'd like that.

The important and the urgent

It's difficult to have fun with someone you never see, someone you don't spend time with. It's hard to love someone you don't know very well and don't have time for. If we have a 'take it or leave it' attitude to God we will never become intimate with him. I'm only as close to God as I want to be and it takes time and effort. Often the urgent things of everyday living overtake the need for the important things.

The urgent is the persistent, pushing demands, such as the copy deadline, or the cooking and cleaning, or the report writing, or the washing and ironing, things which are very necessary but which may not help us to get to know God better. The important things often don't nag at us or demand our attention and it's easy to push them out of the way – things like our relationship with God, our prayer times, communication with family or friends.

The story of Jesus visiting the home of Martha in Bethany illustrates this. Jesus turned up unexpectedly, probably with the twelve disciples in tow, and Martha rushed around to welcome them and make them a meal (Luke 10:39–42). I often wonder how I would feel if thirteen men dropped in for supper unannounced! I have great sympathy for Martha. Perhaps she wanted to make an elaborate meal, as a demonstration of her love, and it seemed urgent. However, she overlooked the fact that Jesus was in her house and it was a special time. That was the most important point at that moment. Mary, on the other hand, made the most of the opportunity, and sat at Jesus' feet to hear him teach. He praised her for that. (Such a good excuse for not doing the housework, don't you think?) Yet how often have I rushed around to do the necessary jobs – and neglected that precious time with Jesus.

The next time Martha and Mary met Jesus was after the death of their brother Lazarus (John 11: 1–45). Martha was told that Jesus was coming and she rushed out to meet him, knowing he could help. She had strong faith in Jesus, she knew he was the Son of God and she trusted him implicitly. When he had scolded her for her busy-ness before, it was not because of a lack of faith. Even when we are full of faith, there is still much to be learnt about the priorities and the practicalities of everyday living.

The third time Jesus visited Bethany was for a planned dinner party in his honour. Lazarus sat at table with him – and who did the cooking? Martha! Mary, meanwhile, did something really special, for which Jesus said she would always be remembered: she poured expensive scent on his feet and wiped them with her hair (John 12:1–8). It was typical of her intuitive and artistic temperament. She sat at Jesus' feet to learn; she fell at his feet when he arrived at the tomb; and she anointed his feet in another dramatic gesture. She understood something of his purposes and what might happen to him, and why she had to do it. The disciples didn't understand the perfume bit at all!

We have much to learn from Mary, especially if we are natural Marthas. Like Jo and Paula in the opening chapter, here are two different types of women, each with things to learn, but each with things which they do best. Jesus had time for them both, and was concerned for both, and he flouted the convention of his time by his dealings with them. So why did he rebuke Martha? And why didn't he rebuke Mary, who was sitting with the men, at the feet of a teacher – both forbidden to women in Jewish culture?

I wonder if Martha had not learnt to distinguish between the urgent and the important, and therefore to sort out her priorities. Those urgent demands can squeeze out the important time with

Jesus. Martha needed to let go on this occasion because the time with Jesus was available just then. This is the tension, of course. The important – prayer, Bible study, time with my husband or with my child – seems as if it can be delayed, while the urgent jobs, the work, demands our attention. The urgent is seen by others, we think, and its imperativeness saps our energies so that we have nothing left for the important. The important is often unseen by others and so we feel we can concentrate on other things. But can anything be more important than time spent with God our Father, to learn to be intimate with him? Several times we read that Jesus went off to spend time alone with the Father, often early in the morning. If he needed to, how much more do we.

Moses rushed up and down Mount Sinai many times to speak with God. He must have been fit! I enjoy walking, especially in hilly countryside, but the thought of having to climb a mountain in order to talk to God, and to have to do that several times, is rather daunting! Moses didn't complain, and presumably it was well worth the effort. What lengths are we prepared to go to in order to spend time with God?

Yet to find the time often seems impossible. Small children wake earlier than you do, however early you wake. Work deadlines have to be met, maybe under contract terms. Food has to be bought, prepared, cooked, eaten; the dog exercised, the car taken to the garage, the garden weeded – the list of urgencies is long.

I have learnt that there is nothing, absolutely nothing, which is as important, as meaningful and as rewarding as time spent with my heavenly Father. When I don't have this time with him every day, I certainly notice the difference.

I once listened to a tape addressed to women about how to make time for what they really wanted to do (and the assumption was that they really wanted to exercise and keep fit but couldn't motivate themselves). The American speaker urged her listeners to get up half an hour earlier each day, before husband or children were awake, and spend that extra time in exercise and fitness training while listening to mind-improving tapes. 'You can do it,' she said. 'I have.' She explained how that extra half an hour had changed her, by energising her, motivating her, giving her the strength to change her whole life. 'Try it for yourself,' she urged. The idea that exercising could change one's whole life seemed to me a flawed one. However, if merely exercising could make that much difference, what would happen if I spent the time with God? If someone could become so motivated over toning and stretching, what do I have to do to get motivated to keep in touch with my heavenly Father?

Finding the time

Half an hour before the rest of the world is awake may be a good time for some, but not for others. You may be an owl rather than a lark, and not function properly until much later in the day. There may be schedules to meet or babies who demand to be fed immediately. It's no good giving God the dregs of your time: neither of you will enjoy the taste. Find the time which suits you and allows you to be at your best with God. Pray about this, talk to him about it, and together work out what will suit you at the moment. You may need to change your schedule many times throughout your life to fit in with the different stages and needs.

A few months ago I prayed about my time with God and found myself waking up at 6.15 am every morning, without an alarm to disturb the slumbering form beside me. It gave me nearly an hour alone with God and I loved it. The time was very special. It energised me for the rest of the day and it led to enormous changes in my life as I discussed things with God. I happen to be a lark, and so an early appointment suits me.

I also need to spend time with God throughout the day. I might sing aloud to praise tapes as I drive to the supermarket. I might pray as I walk the dog. I might learn a verse while I do the ironing. I like to think of him first thing in the morning and last thing at night, perhaps with a prayer or a song or just a 'Good morning, God', 'Good night, Lord'. It's good to be in the habit of constantly being in touch with God and spending each day with him. Even on the days when a longer time with God is not possible, there are the little moments 'touching base'.

You will need prayerfully to find your own best time to be intimate with God. Write it in your diary every day so that nothing can dislodge it. What's in my diary gets done. What's vaguely in my mind gets overlooked.

Finding the place

I have a special place to meet with God. If that makes you envious because you don't live in a large, four-floored, seven-bedroomed, draughty Anglican rectory and so don't have much space, let me assure you that my place with God is special not because it's large but because it's the place where I go to be with him. I always go to that chair in that room, and so as soon as I sit down, I'm expectant and automatically beginning to get in tune with him. It took a while to happen. I tried other places first to see which worked best. For me, looking out of the window was distracting – I could see the weeds and the weather! I need little to look at and nothing to listen to, not even the clock because the tick intrudes. It's just him and me when I go to my chair.

The only place that Liz can be alone with God in her small busy house is the bathroom, so she goes in and locks the door and enjoys five minutes of peace with him.

Finding the intimacy

Reading

I read something from God's word every day. The Bible is the maker's instructions, a map, a love letter and infinitely more besides. Sometimes I use a commentary to help me understand what I've read. I also (but never instead of) read a helpful Christian book or the biography of another Christian. I learn verses from Scripture and I write out my favourites and keep them where I can see them. Were I artistic, I might illustrate them too.

Writing

I keep two journals. One is where I write my thoughts and feelings, descriptions of things I've done and places I've been, notes on books I've read, my dreams and goals and decisions, my walk with God, talks I've heard. I write in it when I feel like it, which is nearly every day but doesn't have to be. It is a record of my spiritual life as well as my everyday life.

The other is my prayer journal, and I have to write it daily. I write out word for word what I want to say to God and then I say it out loud. It is the only way I have found to prevent my mind from wandering. I have a page a day and I divide it into five: Adoration, Confession, Thanksgiving, Supplication and Listening. It was hard to begin with – Supplication wanted to use up most of the page and the first and last sections didn't know where to start.

Adoration

Here are some of the ways I worship God, which you may find helpful:

• Sing a song to God – perhaps a favourite one from church, or a psalm or a song you've made up. This isn't the same as thanking him, that comes later. This is worship and adoration and praise, something which doesn't always come very naturally in our culture.
• Sing aloud.
• Praise God for his attributes: try it alphabetically – Lord you are adorable, brilliant, constant, dynamic, exalted . . . precious . . . zestful!
• Sing in tongues.
• Sing standing up.
• Sing to a praise tape.
• Spend a few minutes (until you find yourself daydreaming) in silent wonder, love and praise.
• Lift your hands or your face to him.
• Sing or say the songs they sing in heaven, eg 'Holy, holy, holy, the Lord God the Almighty, who was and is and is to come . . . You are worthy, our Lord and God, to receive glory and honour and power, for you created all things, and by your will they existed and were created' (Revelation 4:8,11). Some others are in Revelation 5:12–13; 15:3–4.

Don't worry if you can't sing in tune: this is between you and God, and he loves to hear your voice. The psalmist said to make a joyful noise to the Lord! It may sound like a noise to others, but to your heavenly Father it's a sweet sound.

Confession

This may be hard. It isn't a general confession, such as 'God, I'm sorry I'm so dreadful.' This is a specific admitting and confessing, acknowledging the individual things done wrong since the last confession. It's something to do regularly otherwise it takes a long time! We should keep short accounts with God; unconfessed sin causes a barrier between us and our heavenly Father.

'I admit that I lost my temper with Emma . . . I didn't talk about you to Helen when the opportunity arose in conversation . . . I really envied that expensive new dress Jane was wearing . . . I haven't kept close to you throughout the day and . . . and . . . I'm sorry. Please forgive me.'

You might find it helpful to:

• Confess on your knees.
• Confess flat on your face.
• Confess with all your heart, fasting, weeping and mourning (Joel 2:12).
• Acknowledge that God is almighty and perfect and you fall far short of his standards.

He is a God who is ready to forgive, 'gracious and merciful, slow to anger and abounding in steadfast love' (Joel 2:13).

He cleanses and restores and gives us the freedom to start again.

He 'will abundantly pardon' (Isaiah 55:7) no matter what it is that we have done.

He 'blots out' the confessed sins and forgets them (Isaiah 43:25).

He does not bear grudges.

He throws our sins in the sea (Micah 7:19) and it's as if he puts up a sign saying 'No Fishing' – he forgets the confessed sin, and so should we.

Thanksgiving

I like to be specific. Having thanked God for forgiving and cleansing me, I go on to different areas. There may be answers to prayer:

I can go back to where the request was written in the first place, and record his goodness to me. I thank him for friends, family, home and blessings. People I've seen, people who have helped me; times when I have known his power, his presence, his help. '[Give] thanks . . . at all times . . . and for everything' (Ephesians 5:20).

1 Thessalonians 5:18 adds, 'Give thanks in all circumstances.' That always reminds me of the story of Corrie Ten Boom and her sister in a concentration camp during the Second World War. The women's living quarters were heavily infested with lice. Corrie complained bitterly to God but her sister gave thanks, even in that situation. Later, they realised that the infestation meant that their guards wouldn't enter the barracks and so the women were able to talk about God and hold services without interruption. Corrie learnt the hard way to give thanks in every situation, even when infested by lice in a concentration camp.

Thank God for the good things; thank him through and in spite of the difficulties; thank him for the big things and the not so big; and finally, thank him for all he has done for you, from Calvary onwards.

Supplication

This is what so many people think prayer is all about. 'Please God . . . give me this . . . save me from that . . . bless me and my family and my friends . . . .'

Ask first for the wisdom to pray as God directs. You need to know what he wants you to be praying for. If we are truly abiding in him, we begin to know what is on his heart and what is his will. Don't settle for less. Talk to your Father, naturally and without religious clichés. Tell him what is on your heart, and ask what is on his.

I find it helpful to divide my supplication into five main areas.

- My work: what I do, how I do it and when.
- My church: its ministry and outreach, the staff, Sunday services, my involvement.
- My family: my husband, our marriage, our children, our finances, my mother and sister.

- Other people: friends, extended family, missionaries.
- Myself: for God to be at work in me, in my character or attitudes; my daily needs.

I have one list, or rota, for each day of the week and another one for each date of the month. Some things or people I pray for daily, some weekly and some monthly. I pray for specific things which I write down, and then when God answers I can go back and write the date beside it. I use some of Paul's prayers when praying for others (eg Ephesians 1:15–23; Phillipians 1:3–11), and sometimes I will write to tell a friend what I have been praying for her.

Listening

When I've had my say, it's time to listen. I have to write that down as the last thing on my prayer page: time spent in silence waiting on God, listening to him. I haven't found this easy and I need practice. I don't hear a definite voice (although I know other people do) and I don't always feel anything. But the times when I know that it is God communicating with me are so special and so humbling that I'll go on practising.

Finding your style

Gillian paints pictures and illustrates her prayer journal. Janet exercises to Christian dance music and dances before the Lord, as David did. Anne is learning a psalm a month. Lynn is always sending attractive little cards to others who need reminding of God's love for them. Each of my friends has found ways of increasing her intimacy with her heavenly Father, to help when it's difficult and times are dry. I've shared with you ways that I have found very helpful to me; some of it will be encouraging for you and some may not appeal. Not everyone would find it easy to write a journal or read a written prayer to God. Some might want more room for spontaneity, or for quiet contemplation and meditation; some may prefer to use the words of others, such as following one of the liturgical patterns in the *Book of Common Prayer*. What is important is that we each spend time with God, using ways which help and inspire us, which draw us closer to God and which enable the Spirit to work in us.

Accountability

Once a fortnight, my friends and I meet for Bible study and we hold each other accountable. We talk about what God has been doing in our lives, what we have learnt about him, how much time we have spent with him. And we tell one another what we each determine to do before we meet again in order to keep close to God. Knowing that a close friend or two will want to hear how you are getting on with God is a real incentive to put your words into action. Have you thought of meeting regularly, with just one or two friends, to pray together, to support one another and to hold one another accountable?

* * *

A relationship with God is special; it takes time, effort, practice. Its rewards are limitless. 'Hem your day with prayer and it is less likely to come unravelled.'

Putting it into practice

• Meditate on the story of Martha and Mary (John 12:1–8), asking God to speak to you. Can you define the urgent and the important in your life?
• There are several ideas in this chapter to help you in your relationship with God. Choose one or two and work on them.
• How could you make your times alone with God more special and intimate?
• Ask others what they find helpful. Share ideas for increasing intimacy with God.

5

Conflicting Designs

Let each of you lead the life that the Lord has assigned, to which God called you. (1 Corinthians 7:17)

Summer, a couple of years ago. Sue and I lay back in the old-fashioned, striped deck-chairs, basking in the golden sunlight of a late Saturday afternoon in June. The air was warm, the sky a hazy azure. Scents of summer – roses, pinks, mown grass, a barbecue being lit – wafted dreamily past us. We sipped lazily at our drinks, chatted quietly, enjoying the sense of peace and contentment in the large walled garden. It was bliss. 'What a glorious place you've got here!' Sue said half enviously. The vast old house, the walled garden, the small town – all beautiful, just what I'd always wanted. 'We're very spoilt. God's really blessed us,' I agreed.

A year later and I was storming around the house and garden, venting my frustration and anger on anything that got in my way. Any contentment with life had evaporated. I was fed up with things as they were: the house which was so difficult to clean and heat, the perpetual struggling to manage on a small income, the lack of what other friends had. And I was cross that my husband hadn't got a particular job I wanted him to have – he hadn't even applied for it, and I had tried my hardest to persuade him.

What had changed?

Not very much externally, but internally my attitude and state of mind. I had decided I'd had enough, and lost sight of what God had chosen for me, and began wanting my own way. I forgot how God had guided us in the past, and instead of looking at the many blessings he had given to us, I was comparing myself with those who had other blessings. So I lost contentment. I chose to be dissatisfied.

We know we've been specially designed by God and chosen by him; we know that he has wonderful plans for us and that we can have a wonderful relationship with him. But so often, we think we can do better by ourselves. The grass looks greener on the other side and we long to cross over to enjoy the fresh-looking pastures others are enjoying. (The grass on the other side still has to be mown, though, and it too produces moss and weeds.) We look at what others have: maybe their lifestyle or job, their husband or children, their income or their abilities – and we become unhappy with our own circumstances.

Paul wrote, 'I have learned to be content with whatever I have . . . In any and all circumstances I have learned the secret of being well-fed and going hungry . . . I can do all things through him who strengthens me' (Phillippians 4:11–13). Paul said he had *learnt* to be content, so presumably it didn't come naturally to him either. So how can I make the most of where God has put me and what he has made me? How do I learn contentment? It can be very elusive.

Learning to be content

Trusting God in spite of the circumstances

There are many areas of our own lives in which most of us are free to make our own choices. But sometimes we can't. Singleness, childlessness, illness, disability may be forced upon us. How do we learn to trust God then?

One woman learnt in a very hard way – she had been forced by her father to marry a man who didn't love her. And as if that wasn't enough, she then had to see her husband marry a second woman, whom he did love – her younger sister. It must have caused Leah great heartache and grief. Jacob had worked seven years to gain the hand of Rachel, but Rachel's father tricked Jacob into marrying Leah, the older sister. Jacob did not recognise her at the ceremony – presumably she was heavily veiled. Within twenty-four hours, Jacob angrily confronted his father-in-law and persuaded him to let him marry Rachel as well.

How humiliating for Leah, to know she was not the chosen, loved wife. It was the beginning of a lifetime of unhappiness. Over the next few years, Leah was to have six sons and a daughter, while her maid also bore Jacob two sons. Sons were seen as a special blessing from God, so Leah would have been thought very fortunate by others. But what the world perceived was very different to how things actually were. Leah was unloved, in difficult circumstances not of her own choosing. What did she learn about contentment?

The clues are in the names she gave her sons. Their meanings show a deepening relationship with God as she leant on him in her struggles. There was Reuben – see, a son. 'The Lord has seen my misery.' Then came Simeon – one who hears. 'The Lord heard me.' The third son was Levi – attached. 'My husband will become attached.' Judah – praise. 'I will praise the Lord.' There is no record of self-pity, reproaches to God, or anger against Jacob and Rachel, but a reliance on God, bringing her troubles to him, trusting him and praising him. What a positive attitude.

The next son, child of Leah's maid, was Gad – 'What good fortune!' The two sons of Leah's maid counted legally as Leah's, and so she named them both. After Gad was Asher – 'How happy I am, because others will think I am happy!'

But soon, Leah had to buy her husband's company for a night by supplying the childless Rachel with some mandrakes (also called love apples, a symbol of happiness and thought to aid fertility). Leah had another son. Issachar – reward. 'God has rewarded me.'

Leah had been faithful, trusting God in spite of her situation. She took her problems to him, and in difficult circumstances she knew his blessings. Another son followed, Zebulun – honour. 'God has given me a special gift; my husband will honour me.'

It is interesting to see this woman's relationship with God deepen and strengthen, and how the promise of God to Abraham, to make his family into a great nation, was extended through Leah. Jesus was descended from Judah, Leah's son, not from one of Rachel's beloved sons, Joseph and Benjamin. All of humankind has been blessed through Leah. Even though she never had the love of her husband, Leah continued to trust God. And 'God listened to Leah' (Genesis 30:17).

Leah handed her problems to God. He didn't remove them, but he did bless her through them, helped her to cope with them and drew her closer to him. Years later, when Jacob died, he was buried, at his own request, next to Leah in the family vaults (Genesis 49:29–33). Rachel had died years before, giving birth to Benjamin, the last son, and had been buried at Bethlehem. Leah's death is not recorded, but her son is in the genealogy of Jesus – she was part of God's plan for redemption (Matthew 1:2). 'The Lord has seen . . . the Lord has heard . . . I will praise the Lord.' How Leah must have longed for her husband's love, for life to be different, yet she trusted God.

Choosing contentment within the circumstances

Have you ever allowed the weather to get the better of you, let alone large problems like Leah's? Grey sad days, especially in February, can upset my equilibrium and cause me to feel depressed and tired. Small or large, our circumstances can have a profound effect on us if we allow them to. We can choose to be affected by the weather, or we can refuse to be annihilated by it, and carry our own weather within us. If I allow circumstances to dictate to me, aren't I being driven by impulses and feelings, rather than allowing God's design for me to guide me? I can't do anything to change the weather, however much I try, and it's a waste of my time and effort to worry away at things I have no control over. But I can do something about the music group at church, which God has called me to lead. I can take a Bible study at music practice, enthuse and encourage when we sing and play, pray for the members of the group and for our involvement in the Sunday services. When I concentrate my energies into the positive things where I can make a difference for God, the other areas lose their importance.

The weather is one thing; but what if it's something infinitely more important which affects us deep within our hearts – like singleness? What if God's design for you is to remain single at the moment, when everyone around you has a boyfriend or husband? Can you then choose to be content within the circumstances?

All of us are called by God to be single, unless and until we are called to be married. According to Paul, it is the most desirable option for a Christian (1 Corinthians 7:38) and is one of the spiritual gifts. But I wonder how many of us while single have seriously prayed and beseeched God for that gift of celibacy. Most women long to be loved, to be married, to have children; it's part of God's creation design for women. Most women are married, and yet he still calls some to be single, maybe until they're older, maybe for life. The longing in their hearts can't be fulfilled, and I know, from talking with single friends, of their struggles and frustrations. It can be a hard calling, even though in today's society it is perfectly acceptable to remain single, be a career woman, live alone. But for a Christian that also means remaining celibate, which non-believing friends can't understand and may laugh at. Some women may cope, but it's a hard, lonely road, and they long to know the comfort of a husband to protect and cherish and love them.

Influencing others

Two single women have had a great impact on my life. As a teenager, I went to Crusader classes. Every Sunday in term time, Joyce Bates, 'Batty' to us, gave up her Sunday afternoons to tell fifty or so giggly, bored teenage girls the good news about Jesus. In the holidays she took me, the only Crusader day girl, to London, to Crusader reunions. In the morning there would be an outing to Madame Tussaud's or the British Museum. I shall never forget surreptitiously eating the lovely packed lunch she provided while we sat in the back row of the Planetarium, watching the stars roll over our heads. Then, in the afternoons at the reunions, I heard Evelyn Booth-Clibborn, Helen Roseveare, Isobel Macdonald and many others, giving their testimonies. Those were very special times which had a profound effect on my spiritual life. They occurred because a single lady chose to spend her spare time shepherding young girls. It would have been extremely difficult for her to have done so much had she had a husband and family.

The other woman who has been a great influence on me is my godmother. A tall and determined lady, she was headmistress of a primary school, and worked strenuously for God in her local church and in support of missionaries. I wanted to be like her. Jessie decided to have just the one godchild in order to do the job properly – perhaps she realised how difficult a job I presented. Over the years she has faithfully prayed for me – and now for my children too – and I have been very conscious of her support and her prayers. She gave me good advice about boyfriends when I was sixteen, advice which my parents had also given but which I had refused to take from them.

I eventually became a teacher, although never a headmistress; I grew taller than she is, but I never have achieved her level of commitment to her Lord. I, too, have kept to one goddaughter, to concentrate on praying for her. Jessie has been an important part of my life, especially when I was younger, and I am grateful for her example. I know that she could not have done all that she did if she had had a family to look after as well. Now over ninety, she is still working for God. She drives 'old' ladies to services. Being single can be very fruitful, in spite of the lonely circumstances.

Single at the turn of the century?

A young single friend read about Batty and Jessie, and exclaimed, 'But they're old! What about me? I'm still young and unmarried! What can I do? How can I be content when I long to be married?' And there isn't one easy answer. God's calling may seem unreasonable when she is young and attractive and longs to have a husband. How do others cope? Like Leah, they learn to turn to God; to concentrate on areas where they can make a difference for him. But the longing may not be taken from them. It is hard to understand God's reasons. Sometimes, though, it's clear that, like Paul, they are called by God to do something which would be impossible if they were married.

There are two special single women who are part of our

extended family. Wendy is a member of our church, and was one of the youth group leaders. She has played a significant part in the lives of our teenagers. They have shared deep secrets with her that they couldn't tell me; they have wept and laughed with her, and she has prayed with them and for them. She has set them an example in her walk with the Lord. Recently, God called her to missionary work in Cameroon, and my children have seen what it meant to Wendy to hear and respond to God's calling – the joys and excitements, the cost and the sacrifice. They have also seen Wendy and me meeting regularly to read the Bible and pray together. I have cried with Wendy as she saw the man she thought she might marry eventually marry someone else. My teenagers had the privilege of seeing God call Wendy, a single woman in her late twenties, and the difference it made to her as she acknowledged the calling, and embraced it as her gift from God. She's gone to Africa excited, glad to be free to serve God without encumbrance, trusting that he will meet every one of her needs, including loneliness, as she teaches children in different parts of the country. She went apprehensively, not knowing what was in store; and she went sadly, knowing that her parents would really miss her; but she went secure in God, knowing that was where he wanted her. She couldn't do the job of an itinerant teacher were she a married woman.

Sue is in her thirties and works in the media. She breezes in and out of our home in between television appearances, holiday trips to exotic lands or her latest interviewing of celebrities. She brings a touch of glamour to our lives. Since they were young the children have adored her, and have had such fun with her. She's shown them that the Christian life isn't dull and boring, that Christians can work in the arts, and that it's possible to be working on television one minute and helping on a church mission the next. Sue's working lifestyle would be very difficult if she were married.

Both Sue and Wendy, single women, have an important role in our family life. It has been wonderful to have younger women to be influential with my children; and Sue and Wendy value our Christian home which they can be part of and contribute to. At times of loneliness and when in need of emotional support, a Christian family can provide a haven. Families tend to be inclusive and shut out singles, but we gain as much as we give, if not more, by welcoming them, opening our homes to them, including them at weekends and on outings and holidays.

Joyce, Jessie, Sue and Wendy have all found peace and true fulfilment because they have been able to give their lives completely to the service of God. It doesn't mean that the desires for a husband, for married life and for children disappear. It does mean a total dependence on God and trust in him to supply all our needs.

'But,' said Sarah, who is a young single girl, 'being a virgin is very hard in a world that laughs and scorns you for being so, and I'm treated as if it's not been my decision but something forced on me by no one liking me enough to want to sleep with me!' It is hard when the world causes us such pain, and it's then we need to look to God for his comfort, support and strength. It isn't easy; but God does promise that his strength is made perfect in our weakness (2 Corinthians 12:9).

For some, singleness can be better than marriage. The secret is that singleness is a real gift from God and when it is accepted as such, brought to him and left with him, it can bring great blessing to you and to others through you. God may intend you to be single for life, or he may plan a husband for you one day. The important thing is whether you can leave it to him to choose, and that may mean a daily struggle to sacrifice this to him. The examples of single women who have gone before you may help you; listening to God in his word will certainly strengthen you.

Can you rely on his promise: 'None of them that trust in him shall be desolate' (Psalm 34:22, KJV)? 'Yes,' said Sarah. 'It's very challenging, exciting and thrilling. The hard times are still hard, but learning to give it all over to God is a minute-by-minute lesson, with minute-by-minute struggles. But with minute-by-minute rewards.'

Seize the day!

Everything went wrong for one man. His siblings hated him, mostly because he was the favourite son. They tried to get rid of him, and eventually he was taken as a slave to a foreign country. Had he been full of self-pity, bewailing his circumstances which were beyond his control, no one would have been surprised. Instead, he concentrated on being the best he could be for God, and with God's help he worked his way to a top position. Falsely accused and convicted, he had to start from the bottom again, this time in prison. Once more, he soon worked his way up, trusted by his jailers who gave him responsibility. Eventually, he became the Chancellor of Egypt, the man next in authority to Pharoah. Joseph didn't give in to his circumstances, nor did he learn merely to be content with them. He chose to work with them, seizing every opportunity to be the best he could be and enabling God to use him. Eventually God's people, Israel, were saved from famine because of Joseph.

I find that immensely challenging and also very satisfying. When I look back at the end of my life, what will I have achieved for God? Will I have been so tied down by my circumstances that my life has been wasted? How will I have chosen to react to what happens? Mary, Duchess of Ancaster, died on 18 October 1793, and is buried in Edenham Church. Her memorial stone proclaims that her 'death sealed the inimitable virtues of a useful and pious life'. What do I want said about me after my death? What do I want on my tombstone? What's *really* important?

Putting it into practice

'In pursuit of happiness we lose contentment.'

• List what you think will make you happy.
• Compare it with God's values for eternity. What will we be able to take with us when we go to heaven?
• If eternity with God is my goal, what steps should I take now to prepare me for that end?

6

Designed to Be Feminine

Be beautiful inside, in your hearts, with the lasting charm of a gentle and quiet spirit which is so precious to God. (1 Peter 3:4, Living Letters)

The day was perfect – warm sunshine, a soft summer breeze, white clouds in a deep blue sky. As the bride and groom emerged from the church service, they were greeted by showers of confetti and rose petals. It was idyllic. But what captured my attention was the face of Rachel, the bride. She was radiant, her face transformed. From the time she entered the church until the time she and William left for the honeymoon, she didn't stop smiling at him. She glowed with love and happiness.

Recently, I attended a Christian conference for the leaders of an international church organisation. The women there shone – there was an indefinable light and love in their eyes which made a difference. It really does show on our faces if our hearts are in love.

Being feminine

God made us as women – he purposely designed and planned us that way. To be feminine is to be the best we can be. We may think being feminine means being little girlish and kittenish, fluffy, pink and purring. Or, at the other extreme, a roaring tiger who devours men for breakfast. Being feminine is being womanly, the quality of being female, and it encompasses more than individual temperaments. Its essence is attractive and lovable. It comes from the heart and it affects our actions, our appearance and our attitudes.

Feminine actions

A feminine heart attempts the unexpected

Today women have tremendous opportunities and huge potential to do almost anything we choose. Christian women have always been able to do what God called them to do, even when it was difficult, because of the enabling power of his Spirit. Mary Slessor, a Scottish factory girl, was called by God to the coast of West Africa. Her work in ending many tribal abuses, especially the murdering of twin babies, led to her being made a magistrate with full legal powers. Who would have thought that the young untrained woman would end up as an African magistrate!

Helen Roseveare went to the Congo, a fully trained doctor ready to help and heal the sick. Yet she had to design and build the hospital, brick by brick. In spite of her lack of knowledge of the building trade, she learnt to make the kiln to fire the bricks, to mix the concrete, to mitre the asbestos roofing. Then she had to learn the intricacies of motor mechanics in order to keep the ancient mission vehicle on the road! God asked the unexpected of her, and then gave her the power and inspiration she needed when she obeyed him.

Elizabeth Elliot's husband was murdered in Ecuador by Auca Indians, the very men he had spent six years praying for and trying to befriend. It wasn't long before Elizabeth, her toddler and some of the other widows were back in the area to continue the work begun by their husbands. Through them, the Indians first came to know the Lord.

Each of these women stepped outside what was expected of her. They were women who made a difference for God because they had hearts dedicated to him, willing to do whatever he asked of them. They attempted something so great for God that it was doomed to failure unless God was in it. They knew where God was calling them and they obeyed. They are all women who went to foreign lands; but wherever we are, we too can attempt the unexpected for him. Once we know God's purpose for us we can concentrate on what we need to do to achieve that goal. A goal turns a dream into reality. What are the dreams God has laid on your heart? What are you longing to do for him? What unexpected goal might he be calling you to?

If this seems daunting as well as exciting, it can be helpful to consider the steps needed to achieve a particular goal. Perhaps you may feel God wants you to translate the Bible into an unknown language in a far-flung part of the world. What steps would you need to take to get there and start work? You'd think of training, applications, money, freeing yourself of ties, research. Then break it down into the different stages and work out the time-scale for each. You'd plan it all very carefully.

Or maybe you feel God calling you to form a drama group at church. Your plan might look like this:

Pray!

Talk to the minister about it: fix date.

Find two or three others who are interested: arrange for notice on the weekly sheet.

Arrange initial meeting together: fix time and place.

Order book of scripts from church bookstall.

Begin working together and rehearsing: fix regular times.

Whatever your dream, list all that will be necessary to achieve it and put it into a logical sequence. Be realistic about the time involved and the time available, and work out each step for the next few weeks and months. Before you know it, you will have achieved your goal.

A feminine heart works hard for the Lord

Housework makes me very cross! No sooner have I finished dusting the furniture than a thin film reappears on it. Or I iron a garment beautifully – and a day or two later it's back in the wash again. It seems such a waste of time. However, I have learnt that I can use the time productively. It all depends on my motivation. If I want 'to honour the Lord and bring good to others', like the hard-working woman of Proverbs 31, then I will view the work in a different light. I can pray about the people who will be in that room; I can pray for the member of the family whose clothes I'm ironing; I can sing my praises to God at full voice while I use the vacuum cleaner and no one will complain at my tunelessness.

Not everyone hates housework. You may dislike gardening, or the filing in the office, or the travelling to work. Whatever you have to do, bring it to God each time and do it motivated by his praise and glory. That doesn't happen overnight: like most things it takes practice. But it's well worth the effort.

A feminine heart reaches out to others

A teenage girl who loved swimming dived into the inviting water – and very nearly didn't surface again. She was pulled to safety by others, who rushed her to hospital. It soon became apparent that she would never walk again, and she spent many months in hospital as they tried to alleviate the symptoms of quadraplegia as much as possible. Joni Eareckson went through a time of great pain and frustration, but she clung to God through it all. New talents emerged: she began to paint using her mouth, to sing, and to write. Her books, often illustrated with her own beautiful line drawings, have become international best sellers and have been used by God to help and inspire many other people. In spite of severe disabilities which make her totally dependent on others, God uses her to encourage, challenge and strengthen others. 'Encourage one another and build up each other' (1 Thessalonians 5:11). We can do that in many different ways.

After I had had major surgery, inevitably I was weak and feeble for a while, but I was helped by other women who reached out to me in the power of the Spirit. Eleanor laid hands on me and prayed for swift healing – and I was walking the dog within two weeks, not the three months the consultant had advised at first. Jennie cooked a delicious meal for my family, even though she's got her own young family to look after. Mo came regularly for several weeks to iron and clean, even though she's a working woman.

We encourage others when we do things for them, pray, share ourselves, take time to be with them. We build them up when we want the best for them, when we forgive and forget any hurt and refuse to gossip, when we share what God has been doing in our lives and what he can do in theirs. Reach out to others for God and our own life will be immensely enriched as well.

A feminine appearance

A feminine heart is filled with the Spirit

'Look to him and be radiant; so your faces shall never be ashamed' (Psalm 34:5). However fashionable or unfashionable we are, however groomed and gorgeous, there is nothing we can do to prevent the final decay of our earthly bodies, but the beauty of a woman in love with Jesus is unfading. Being beautiful from the heart should be the core of our femininity. Think of the difference to be seen in the faces of two women, one bitter and angry, the other loving and patient. Internal feelings affect what others see when they look at us. Frowning is bad for the face and produces wrinkles. Laughing makes you feel better, exercises the right muscles and produces facial character.

We women, whether kittens, tigers or something in between, are specifically reminded that our real beauty comes from the 'unfading loveliness of a calm and gentle spirit' (1 Peter 3:4) which is the essence of the Spirit of God at work in us. As we spend time with God, he produces his fruit in us: love, joy and peace; patience, kindness, goodness, faithfulness, gentleness and self-control. Then our love for the Lord is seen in our faces. It works from the inside out.

Lots of beauty preparations try to improve the face – they allegedly help to reduce wrinkles and fine lines and make the skin look more radiant. But they can only make a surface difference; eating a healthy diet and drinking pints of water each day actually have a greater effect because they work from the inside. In the same way, you can change your appearance and even attempt to alter your behaviour, but it will be a surface difference only unless God changes your heart. The glorious thing is that he wants to. He has promised to fill us with his Spirit: 'I will pour out my Spirit on all people . . . Even on my servants, both men and women, I will pour out my Spirit in those days' (Joel 2:28–29, NIV).

Angela and John were staying with us for the weekend when John was taken ill and rushed into hospital. Angela was shocked and worried, but she prayed and trusted God. While John was in intensive care, Angela relied totally on God. Her heart was fixed on him and nothing could shake that, and it showed on her face. Her confidence was in a God who was in charge of the situation.

When being pursued by Saul, who wanted to kill him, David wrote, 'My heart is fixed, O God, my heart is fixed: I will sing and give praise' (Psalm 57:7, KJV). Life was tough for David, but he was fully confident in God: 'Be merciful, O God, for my soul trusteth in Thee: yea, in the shadow of Thy wings will I make my refuge, until these calamities be overpast' (Psalm 57:1–2, KJV). If our hearts are fixed on God, when life jolts us we will not be caught unawares.

Moses reflected God, too. After Moses had been talking with God, he had to wear a veil over his face because the light shining from him was too dazzling for others to look at (Exodus 34:29–35). When our trust is in God, it shows. It gives a special kind of beauty to our faces.

A feminine heart has lasting beauty

I love wearing pearls, in my ears, around my neck. The special ring my husband gave me is a sapphire. My teenage daughters have silver bracelets, rings, necklaces. Margaret always wears a cross with unusual turquoises on it. Nancy loves rubies and Anne has huge gold earrings. Most of us have special clothes for special occasions. But Paul wrote, 'Women should dress themselves modestly and decently in suitable clothing, not with their hair braided, or with gold, pearls or expensive clothes' (1 Timothy 2:9). Peter echoed the sentiment in 1 Peter 3:3: 'Do not adorn yourselves outwardly by braiding your hair, and by wearing gold ornaments and fine clothing.' What does that mean for us at the turn of the century when women can be seen in almost anything – or almost nothing? Culturally, there are big differences between the acceptable dress of two thousand years ago and today. Then, a woman of low repute would have had long loose hair, which was shaved off if she was found out. Now, women of the red light districts are 'dressed to kill'. In the Graeco-Roman world, women wore a veil as a symbol of submission and propriety. Wealthier women flaunted their status with lots of expensive and ornate jewellery.

Fashion, make-up, jewellery are of secondary importance, but they should help us to look our best. They should not distract others nor tempt the opposite sex. They should not bring the name of Jesus into disrepute through ostentation, vanity, immodesty or carelessness. And they should be well within our budgets. We can dress to honour God, who is interested in how we look – he made us, after all.

Some of the women in the Bible took great care over their appearance. Ruth, instructed by her mother-in-law, had a bath, sprayed on her favourite perfume and carefully selected her best dress before going to see Boaz. Esther had twelve months of beauty treatments and chose her outfit wisely before asking her husband the king for a favour. 'Whatever you do, do everything for the glory of God. Give no offence' (1 Corinthians 10:31–32).

Mother Theresa from Romania wore Indian saris as she worked among the poor of Calcutta. Isobel Kuhn from Canada wore the clothes of the Lisu tribe in Thailand. They adapted to the fashion culture of the people they wanted to win for Christ because they didn't want clothes to be a barrier by being different and calling attention to themselves. The external appearance should not be the main concern in our lives, nor the primary cause of our beauty, but it should be the best we can be for God.

Feminine attitudes

Equal but different

Femininity is not a rival of masculinity and it doesn't have to be compared with masculinity. Being feminine is being what God intended for us as women, with hearts filled with his Spirit. Femininity is living out God's principles in our lives.

Men and women were created equal, because both were made equally in the image of God. They were told to look after creation together. He was to cleave to her, she was to bear children, and they were physically different. But together they became one flesh and both were needed. She was his helper, to meet his needs because he was lonely and nothing else in creation would do. Helper does not imply inferiority – God is described as Israel's helper (Psalm 115:9) and the Holy Spirit is our helper (Philippians 1:19). Man on his own is not self-sufficient; woman is complementary. They complete each other; and their happiness depends on each asking for and receiving what only the other can give.

At the foot of the cross we are equal – sinners in need of a saviour. There is an end to discrimination because 'there is no longer male and female; for all of you are one in Christ Jesus' (Galatians 3:28). We are all beloved children of God, heirs together of the grace of God. Equality is not undifferentiated sameness. Knowing that we are equal but different, affects our attitude to men and gives us the freedom to demonstrate the true spirit of servanthood – not insisting on our rights but concentrating on our God-given responsibilities.

Gentle and quiet

A woman who was a natural 'tomboy' as a child, or a woman who is extrovert and flamboyant, appears at first to be the opposite of the woman with a 'gentle and quiet spirit' which Peter had in mind when he wrote to the early Christian women. He said this spirit had an unfading loveliness, which is what we would all like. How do we measure up to this standard of beauty in God's word?

A gentle spirit

There are those who are naturally physically gentle and there are those who are more like the proverbial bull in a china shop. The 'gentle spirit' does not refer to our physical temperament, but to the attitude of our hearts. A gentle spirit is humble before God and wants him to get all the glory. Such a woman is humble in her attitude to others, forgiving, always seeing the best in them. Her opinion of herself is humble; she doesn't always have to be right or have the last word. A gentle spirit is 'patient and kind; is not jealous, or conceited or proud; is not ill-mannered or selfish, or irritable; does not keep a record of wrongs; is not happy with evil, but is happy with the truth . . . never gives up; its faith, hope and patience never fail.' Just like love (1 Corinthians 13:4–7, TEV). A 'me first' frame of mind leads to pride, arrogance, to being judgemental, and to gossip.

Two women were at the Young Wives' prayer meeting. Charlotte has a very comfortable lifestyle, with the elegance and self-confidence which that can give. She prayed, 'God, thank you that I'm not like others. Thank you that I'm not a shop-lifter or a drug-addict. Thank you that I can fast on Monday lunch-time while the au pair looks after the baby. Thank you that I can make such wonderful cakes for the church bazaar.' Meanwhile, Sharon, who lives on the estate and dresses à la jumble sale rather than à la mode, was praying very quietly, covering her face with her hands to try to hide the tears. 'God, I am so sorry. Please have mercy on me. I know I've failed you.'

Jesus told that story (but the characters were a Pharisee and a tax collector who prayed in the Temple [Luke 18:9–14]) to show that the person who pleaded for forgiveness was the one who went home forgiven and justified, 'for all who exalt themselves will be humbled, but all who humble themselves will be exalted' (Luke 18:14).

A quiet spirit

Katie is a very shy and retiring person; she doesn't say much, preferring to remain in the background. Eleanor, on the other hand, always has lots to say, is wildly enthusiastic and her conversation is liberally peppered with superlatives. Yet both of them have a 'quiet spirit'.

The woman with a quiet spirit has harmony and stability in her life. She has an air of being at ease with herself because her confidence is in God and not in her appearance or her age or her designer perfume. She is soothing and peaceful to be with – even if she naturally talks non-stop – because you feel better, encouraged, closer to God, after spending time with her. Her inner being is so immersed in the Lord that her outer presence is glorifying to him and others can see and sense that, and it draws them to him.

I went for an early morning walk with Eleanor. We were at a conference in a lovely part of Sussex, and we were able to wander through dew-drenched fields with oast houses glinting in the early sunlight. It was magical. We talked and talked – or at least Eleanor did. For nearly an hour, she talked and enthused and informed. With anyone else I might have felt exhausted or over-whelmed, but I found it a privilege to listen to her. Whether she was talking about specifically Christian things or not, she radiated love for Jesus, confidence in him and his work in her life. I found myself wanting to learn from her because I could sense her quiet spirit and her assurance of God. It was encouraging – she made me want to press on in my spiritual journey and imitate her because she imitates Jesus.

A spirit which is precious to God

Mrs Clark always came to the evening service at our church. A small, elderly, grey-haired lady, she beamed and twinkled and exuded a 'quiet and gentle spirit'. She was mischievous, quite wrinkled and becoming disabled, but she had had a lifetime of knowing and loving her Lord – and it showed! The gentle and quiet spirit is what will never pass or fade or grow old. This spirit will, in fact, grow better and stronger with use. It is good practice for eternity because it is building holiness in us. Holiness is living according to God's standards and working out how those stan-dards apply to us. Holiness comes from trying to please God, not from trying to please others or conforming to the world's idea of beauty.

Putting it into practice

• Do I honestly want to be appreciated for what I am? Or for what I look like?

• How am I tempted to impress other Christians?

• How much of my time and money do I or should I spend on the outward appearance?

• How do I decide in relationship to my femininity what is bene-ficial and will build up my faith and that of others? (1 Corinthians 10:31 – 11:1)

7

Marriage by Design

A good wife who can find? She is far more precious than jewels. (Proverbs 31:10, RSV)

Picture a busy career woman working long hours in the office, where things are going from bad to worse. Creditors pressing hard, franchisees causing problems, more work than the staff can realistically cope with. At home, the builders are turning everything upside down supposedly to create the house of her dreams, while the nanny suddenly announces that she's taking the whole month off to have an extended holiday. The husband is also busy in a job which involves a lot of travelling away from home, but he runs the financial side of his wife's business on top of his own job, and is worried about the losses it has begun to make. His escape route is to spend any spare time he has on the golf course, taking out his frustrations on a small white ball. The couple drift further and further apart, as the worry and stress cause each of them deep unhappiness which they find hard to express or admit even to one other.

Late one afternoon he phones her at the office to say that yet again he is off to play golf after work and won't be back for supper after all – and the tone of his voice expresses his relief at not having to eat with the family. His wife is furious, feeling not only personally rejected, but also that everything is left to her to deal with – she can't suddenly spend the evening on the golf course because she has a home with a young family awaiting her the minute she leaves the office. So she spits at him over the phone, 'Don't bother to come home – I just might not be there anyway!' He responds immediately, 'Fine; I won't come then.' And they both slam down their receivers. Was this what they thought would happen when they enjoyed a glorious wedding day some years before?

Picture another scene, this time in France on New Year's Eve, in a small hotel miles from anywhere. It is a converted abbey, and retains the beauty and tranquillity of its former glory. There is a gala dinner; course follows course of magnificent French cooking, and at the corner table a couple are obviously spending the most wonderful evening, dancing between courses, holding hands across the table, gazing adoringly at each other with eyes for no one else. Eventually, in the small hours, they slip away to their room upstairs, leaving the party in full swing, and enjoy a romantic night, almost better than any honeymoon.

Two different marriages? Not at all; the valley experience and the mountain-top enjoyment are both true descriptions of our marriage. The depths of despair (fortunately, he did come home, and I was there waiting; we held each other close as we realised the enormity of what we had said, and apologised to one another) was followed a few years later by the blissful short break we managed when the children were all on Christian houseparties over the New Year. Like most marriages, ours has its ups and downs, and there have very occasionally been times when we wish we'd never set eyes on each other, and other times when it's been magical. If you are married, you too may know that there is nothing as devastating or painful as the moments when it all seems to fall apart, when you are pulling in opposite directions, when the love seems to have gone, when you wish you had never set eyes on him. But you may hopefully also know that there is nothing on earth as wonderful as those moments of marriage when it works; when the deep love is there between you, when you understand each other, laugh or cry together, enjoy things together, spend a magical evening together.

A Victorian manual, *Happy Homes and How to Make Them*, gave a list of fifteen rules, the first of which is, 'Don't expect too much.' That isn't how a bride feels on her wedding day! I probably owed more to Walt Disney's song 'Some day my prince will come'. Here he was, and I thought we were going to disappear into the sunset and live happily ever after! Like most brides, I had high, romantic expectations: ours would be a marriage that was happy and wonderful after this glorious beginning. After all, we were deeply in love. But marriage for a lifetime is the day-to-day living along-side another imperfect human being, with the pressing, often mundane, sometimes boring, routines of everyday life. How can a woman who wants to be the best for God and make a difference for him put that into practice in her marriage? How can we try to be examples to other women – to our daughters, to younger Christians, to those we are shepherding – to show them what God designed when he chose to create marriage for us by giving Adam the joy of a wife? And she was a great joy: when he saw her, he was so overcome, he said the equivalent of 'Wow!' He was thrilled; but the bliss of that first marriage was short-lived, and sadly so it is for many marriages today. What can we women do to protect our marriages, to retain the delight we knew when we married the handsome prince who carried us off on our wedding day? How can we stay faithfully married for life and still have fun?

Aren't Christian marriages different?

As you've discovered, my marriage hasn't always been moonlight and roses by any means. Just a few years ago we hit another bad patch. We had young teenagers, stresses in both of our jobs, finan-cial problems – and forty had arrived! Things got so bad that I even thought of moving out just to have some space, and I searched the local paper to see how much it would cost to rent a room, a flat, somewhere to escape. I don't think I am unique in this. Many Christians experience times of dryness and difficulties in their marriages. Just because we go to church, or read the Bible, or pray does not make us exempt from the problems. Indeed, sometimes I think it exacerbates them because we have such high expectations for ourselves, or feel we ought to be able to cope and we can't admit to the difficulties. But there are times when we can't cope. Perhaps a husband is working long hours and seems to have no time for his wife; or he's always on the golf course or at the pub with his friends; or he's at church meetings night after night. She nags because the marriage hasn't turned out the way she hoped and neither has he. Perhaps they fight, verbally or physically, and it's painful and tiring and it drives them apart. Maybe he's having a mid-life crisis – or she is. The children are tiny and crying all night, or they're teenagers and out all night, or they've left home and there's nothing to hold the marriage together any more. Then, we ask ourselves, why stay? No one else does these days . . . we'd both be happier if one of us left . . . I owe it to myself to enjoy life and I'd enjoy it more without him . . . .

What makes a marriage last for life? I have found that there are three things which have proved very helpful to think about: my time, my love and my commitment.

A wife makes time for her husband

Togetherness is very important to a young couple in the early stages of 'going out' and they will spend many evenings doing special things – a meal out, the cinema, a romantic walk. But once married, other demands on our time seem to take precedence. Even when he suggests an evening doing something together, I can have too many other things to be used as an excuse, like the ironing, the children's packed lunches, a letter to write.

When I am stirring a saucepan over a gentle heat, I hate to be distracted. So when my husband comes into the kitchen while I'm cooking, puts his arms around my waist and starts talking to me, I fear he does not have my undivided attention. Far from it; I'll probably wriggle uncomfortably, or mutter crossly that I'm busy. It must be very off-putting for him! I have to learn that giving my time as a gift to my husband, whether it's two minutes of my undivided attention, or an evening to watch his favourite programme with him, is time well spent, invested into my marriage.

Two of our friends actually write in their diaries their time together. They lead busy lives so they are very disciplined, and pencil in one evening a week and one day a month for each other. They may go out or they may stay at home, but it is their time together, for talking, praying, catching up with news, views and

problems. Lack of communication can be one of the biggest difficulties within a marriage. If my husband and my marriage are
important to me, and they are, then I will be prepared to be flexible and fit in time to be with him. Funnily enough, before our marriage, I would have moved heaven and earth in order to be with
him.

Time to pray together is special too. Apart from anything else,
it's very difficult to be angry and rebellious with someone you
pray with regularly. Coming together before God and in his presence creates a very special relationship. Praying together as a
married couple is a unique experience, but is often overlooked in
the busyness of everyday lives. Helen and Tim spend the first five
minutes of every day reading a verse from the Bible and then
praying together. They sit in bed, waiting for the kettle to boil for
the early morning cup of tea, and pray for the coming day, their
children and each other. It's only five minutes, but Helen said it
has made such a difference to their marriage, especially when
there have been difficulties.

A wife is loving to her husband

LOVE BUILDS UP

A young couple came to lunch with us a little while ago. They
haven't been married very long but already she was showing signs
of nagging him. She criticised him in front of us for the way he was
eating, she corrected his statements and she generally put him
down in front of us. It was embarrassing. 'A quarrelsome wife is
like a constant dripping' (Proverbs 19:13, NIV). Why does a
woman work so hard to change a man's habits and then complain
he's not the man she married?

A wife should be her husband's biggest fan, encouraging him,
supporting him, showing that she values and accepts him. She can
build him up by encouraging him, forgiving him his little irritat-
ing foibles and faults, thanking him, and generally being positive
in her attitude. Never underestimate the power of a woman,
declares a sticker I have at home. It's true – we are immensely powerful and we can use that power either to help and to encourage,
or we can use it to break down and ultimately destroy. Nothing

destroys a man's self-esteem more than a domineering woman. 'Better to live on a corner of the roof than share a house with a quarrelsome wife' (Proverbs 25:24). One of the problems today is that men are scared to been seen to be head of the marriage. They have abdicated their position and women easily step in, take over and then undermine them even further by a taunting attitude. I can choose to give my husband the gift of my belief in him, or I can drag him down with snide comments which undermine his confidence, in spite of his masculine appearance of strength. 'A knowing wife, if she is worth her salt, can always prove her husband is at fault,' wrote Chaucer in 'The Wife of Bath's tale'. And so we can – we are very good at putting the knife in, proving him to be in the wrong. It starts with the small, niggly complaints. 'He never washes up; he always leaves his clothes in a heap on the floor; he isn't good at this like so-and-so's husband is.' A negative mind-set quickly finds fault, and the complaints grow.

Ephesians 5:20 tells us to give thanks for everything. Sometimes it helps to make a list of what we like about our husbands and give God thanks for them, concentrating on the positive instead of always seeing the negative. Next week, make a new list. Soon there's not enough space to list all the wonderful things about the man you fell in love with and married. We have a secret weapon, of course. We should never ever stop praying for our husbands. When he wakes you up with his snoring at night, before you thump him and make him turn over, pray for him. Lay hands on him while he is asleep, pray over him and ask God to bless him and pour his favour on him.

LOVE SUBMITS

We had a real dilemma after we had been married for a year. My sister, at that time not a Christian, had decided to get married, but for various reasons my parents were not at all happy with the situation. In the end there was one of those sad family splits and the wedding was planned to take place at the home of the groom. My parents were not invited and my father made it quite plain that I should not go to the wedding. But my sister asked my husband to lead the prayers at the service and he thought it was important that we should both go. I was torn between my husband and my father – both strong characters! On this occasion, I had to learn to submit to my husband and obey him. A husband and wife have a mutually exclusive relationship and it was right for me to do as my husband wanted. In fact, later we were very glad to have been praying at that wedding, and I could see that my husband was right to insist.

All Christians are told to 'be subject to one another out of reverence for Christ' (Ephesians 5:21). In marriage, this means in practice that wives are to 'be subject to your husbands as you are to the Lord' (Ephesians 5:22), and husbands are to love their wives in the same way that Christ loved the Church and gave his life for her. For some of us, the alarm bells will immediately start to ring. Be *subject* to my husband? Submission within marriage is not popular today, perhaps because it is linked with ideas of weakness, inferiority, obedience or control. Isn't it rather risky to relinquish one's authority to someone else, not knowing all that may be involved over the years?

But submission does not mean being a doormat. Submission is having the strength of character to 'cease or abstain from resistance' (*Shorter Oxford Dictionary*). Over the years, I have resisted; I have fought my corner and argued and tried to be the dominant partner. Or I have gritted my teeth and acted out of duty, not love. Yet I can honestly say that I have been most contented and our marriage has worked best when I have been strong enough to submit and put my husband into his rightful place as the head of the marriage. He may not always be right; he may not always be perfect; but he is my husband and so I do as God asks me and I submit to my husband out of reverence for Christ, as Christians do to one another. This is not defeat; this is the glorious affirmation of who God intended me to be as the wife of my husband. I choose, voluntarily, to submit to a lover, not to a monster, because I love him.

LOVE HAS FUN
Do you remember your honeymoon night? Can you recall the hours, days, weeks you had spent getting ready so that you were

at your most attractive on your wedding day? My journal records the exercise routine I followed for several months, the visits to the hairdresser and the chiropodist and the dress-maker. It also joyfully notes the special clothes I bought and the perfume I chose, all in order to make myself especially glamorous for my new husband. The sense of anticipation and the careful planning were enormous! But by the time we arrived at the hotel, we were exhausted at the end of the weeks of planning for the wedding and the long exciting day followed by the driving. You can guess the rest!

Then, a few years later, there were the nights when I crawled into bed exhausted after days of nappies, toddler tantrums and housework, when I felt I'd hardly seen my husband for weeks because of the demands of his busy job, and the last thing I wanted to do was have a night of passion! I craved a long deep sleep, hopefully without a baby crying to wake me up, and felt misunderstood if my husband wanted something else. In Woody Allan's film *Annie Hall* there is a wonderful scene where Woody Allan and Diane Keaton are separately describing their problems to psychiatrists who ask how often the couple make love. He says that it's hardly ever – maybe three times a week. She says that it's all the time, maybe three times a week! We all have different expectations, and sex is important to some, particularly men, and not to others. Yet it can be powerful and healing in a marriage; or energising; or tremendous fun; a place to escape the demands of everyday life and a place to be truly oneself.

Good sex doesn't always happen spontaneously, and it can be planned, worked at and always improved. If you want a passionate Friday night, you sometimes need to plan for it from Monday morning; women are good at planning like that. Little hints are subtly dropped into conversations, creating anticipation, or it's mentioned in a phonecall if one partner is away; the evening is cleared in the diary; maybe some new underwear chosen to create a surprise! It can be such fun – no one else knows what's being planned. Physically demonstrating love can help to keep a marriage alive – be creative and practise being unpredictable. Remember all the weeks of preparation for the honeymoon?

Choosing to spend even ten minutes a day now pampering your-self or exercising will soon pay dividends as you look and feel better. A wife can put fun into sex – he'll love it.

A wife is committed to her husband

A PROMISE

I promised, at our wedding, that with God's help our marriage would last until death parts us. The vicar asked me, 'Will you have this man for your wedded husband . . . Will you love, honour and keep him?' And I replied, 'I will.' Not, I do. I do love him now – it was obvious I did; or I do for a bit until the feeling goes. I promised I will love him, a definite choosing to love in the future. Love in the marriage vow is a verb, an action not a feeling. Feelings may or may not last. A promise is a promise. I promised when I was in my right mind, when I knew and meant what I said, and there were no 'cop-out' clauses such as 'provided he continues to love me, keeps me in the style I'd like to be accus-tomed to, is always young and handsome'. Quite the opposite, in fact; I promised to remain faithful to him no matter what. For better, for worse; for richer, for poorer; in sickness and in health; to love, cherish and to obey. That's what I promised. Shouldn't women of integrity keep their promises, even when it's tough? The world doesn't. The world says it's all right to break a promise. But I want to live my life by God's standards and he is a God who always keeps his promises (Hebrews 10:23) so I want to keep mine too.

I can't do that alone. Sometimes a wife may get fed up with her husband. Many of us experience deep anger, real barrenness, dreadful times which we would not want to admit to others. But God, when I ask, can change me, he can change the situation, and he can renew the love again. 'I can do all things through him [Christ] who strengthens me' (Philippians 4:13). It may not happen overnight. It may mean saying, 'I choose to keep my promise even though I don't feel like doing so, the situation seems too bad to be resolved, I don't feel love any more.' But I can keep my promises because he gives me the grace and strength to do so, even when I'm tempted to give up.

BEING FAITHFUL

We were watching *Pride and Prejudice* on television, and Mr Darcy was darkly stalking across the screen. He was tall, dark and handsome – or so my daughters thought. 'Do you fancy him too?' they asked me. Well, he wasn't bad looking, and he is supposed to be a romantic hero. And it is only a bit of fun to laugh about it like that. But thinking along those lines can be dangerous, and comparing our husbands unfavourably with others causes negative feelings. 'Do not let loyalty and faithfulness forsake you; bind them around your neck, write them on the tablet of your heart' (Proverbs 3:3). Love and faithfulness, for God and for my husband, go hand in hand. I can choose to be faithful, to have eyes only for my husband; or I can allow myself to think about others, to let my eyes wander, to encourage thoughts and daydreams. The idea of 'binding on the neck' and 'writing on the tablet of the heart' reminds me about loyalty and faithfulness. Every time I look at my wedding ring, which is perhaps the modern equivalent of binding on the neck, it's a reminder of the importance of my marriage, of the promises I made, and of the love we have shared together starting in those early days. Personally, if I feel tempted to daydream about another man, I have only to look at his socks and shoes to be frightened off – such unglamorous appendages!

WORDS AND ACTIONS

Family, friends, children, younger women, all see and hear how I treat my husband. Actions as well as words can give a strong message, and show others whether I am committed or not. There have been many evenings, when we have been having supper with others, when I have tried to look good by 'scoring' against my husband, making little jokes at his expense, trying to make myself look cleverer than he is. It may have made me feel successful for a minute or two, but it left a bitter after-taste, and often made me feel rather small. I have learnt the hard way that behaviour like that undermines a marriage and doesn't do much for one's self-esteem in the long run either. So now I try never to run my husband down in public, never to sneer or scoff, never to undermine him.

When I told my husband (at 1.30 am in the course of a 'discussion' on all this!) that I had realised that I was supposed to act towards him as if I was married to Jesus, he was, in his own words, 'gutted'. He felt he had an enormous responsibility. But that is what I felt it said in Ephesians 5:22: 'Submit to your husbands *as to the Lord*' (italics mine). I should behave to my husband as I would to Jesus, I should act towards him as if he was Jesus. What a staggering thought! One to muse over when I shout at him, or hurl a wet dishcloth because I'm cross. It is a very powerful image and deeply affects the way I behave towards my husband.

It's hard and we can't do it by ourselves, but the verse in Ephesians 5 which tells us to behave to our husbands as to the Lord is actually part of a single and much longer sentence in the original Greek. It begins by telling us to be filled with the Spirit, to sing songs and give thanks to the Lord for everything. When we are filled with the Spirit, he works in us to produce his fruit. 'Love, joy, peace, patience, kindness, generosity, faithfulness, gentleness, self-control' (Galatians 5:22–23). Any one of those qualities can revitalise a marriage, but we are promised all of them, if we want them. I find it helpful to pray specifically for this fruit to be found in my life in general, and in my marriage in particular.

COMMUNICATION

Sometimes it seems very difficult to communicate with the opposite sex! I often say, 'The dishwasher is full,' by which I mean, 'Darling, the dishwasher needs emptying. Please could you do it?' But he doesn't understand and walks away, so I think he is being deliberately unco-operative and leaving me to do *all* the household chores, not just this one, yet again. But he tells me that I made a simple statement, which did not require any action. Or he thinks I'm implying that he does nothing to help and I'm criticising him. Another time when I'm feeling really unhappy, he'll ask me what's wrong. 'Nothing,' is always the answer, by which I really mean, 'Everything! Surely you know exactly what's wrong without my having to tell you?' I certainly don't expect him to believe me and turn away.

Either we're not very good at speaking English to one another, or we have the same problem that many others have: we don't communicate what we really mean. After reading *Men are from Mars, Women are from Venus* by John Gray, I learnt that I needed to ask for support and help. 'Darling, please could you empty the dishwasher?' is a magical sentence. It never fails. By rephrasing my sentence into a direct request, I get the help I need, and he feels he has an opportunity to show his love and be a good husband. Good communication is important in any relationship, but I have to work at it in my marriage. I've also learnt not to start what to me is a very important conversation if he is reading the paper or watching sport. It's far more effective if I ask, 'Please may we have five minutes to talk when you've finished?' I'm beginning to learn his language!

Several years ago we planned to stay with some distant cousins who are French, living in a wonderful part of Provence. I was determined to speak a little French by the time we went on holiday, so in the September ten months before I joined a French conversation class. I was so committed to my desire to learn that I stuck with the weekly classes for three whole terms! I did the written homework, I watched French films on television and I listened to the tapes which went with the course. Actually, when we got to France, they spoke perfect English which they insisted on using and I hardly spoke a word of French. But I had tried; I had worked hard because I enjoyed it and because I had a goal. My French, however, had improved only slowly. It takes time to learn a new language, and lots of practice. In my marriage, not only have I had to learn a new language, which takes time, patience, effort, determination, I've had to unlearn the old one as well. But because my goal is to improve my communication with my husband, I'm committed to doing it – and I'm getting there slowly.

ALL YOU NEED IS LOVE

So went the title of a popular song in my childhood. Actually, I think it's true, but I'd probably define 'love' very differently. Each of the definitions of a wife have shown her to have a powerful, deep, determined kind of love. God has designed women to be capable of great emotion, and to be able to fight to protect and keep what they want. We can choose, as married women, to nurture and build that kind of love for our husbands, to build lasting marriages, to be faithful until death parts us. It takes time, love and commitment. It's what we were thinking of doing on the day we were married, although we had no idea of the risk and adventure involved in the future!

When the dog dies and the children leave home, will your marriage be strong and loving for all the exciting years still to come? Will you have built firm foundations so that your marriage can withstand whatever lies ahead? Will you still love him when he's sixty-five?

Putting it into practice

• Thank God for your husband, your marriage and your love. Ask God to give you a lasting love for your husband. List two or three good things about your husband and give thanks for them.

• 'Be subject to one another out of reverence for Christ. Wives, be subject to your husbands as you are to the Lord' (Ephesians 5:21–22). Meditate and pray over these verses.

• Practise telling your husband one positive, encouraging thing each day, to build him up.

• Plan a special surprise evening for your husband and intoxicate him! (See Proverbs 5:18–20.)

8

Designed to Love

He sat down, called the twelve, and said to them, 'Whoever wants to be first must be last of all and a servant of all.' (Mark 9:35)

I lost a favourite, tiny, blue ear-ring the other day. In my anxiety to find it, I turned the bedroom upside down, starting with the box where I keep my 'jewels', then hunting on the floor, under the bed, in the bed, in the jumper drawer, down the stairs, through the kitchen . . . but all to no avail. I was upset. I bought the ear-rings while on holiday abroad, and they exactly match some favourite clothes. I couldn't replace them easily. Eventually, I retraced my footsteps of the previous day, into town to the shop where I had tried on a dress. To my amazement, the ear-ring had been spotted by the assistant while hoovering the floor that morning and it was returned to me. I was overjoyed.

If you have ever searched for something precious and irreplaceable which you've lost, you'll know what it feels like to look frantically everywhere and anywhere. Paul, writing to the church at Corinth, says that love should be searched for like this: 'Pursue love,' he advises (Corinthians 14:1); search hard, don't give up until you've found it.

Love is . . .

I love sunshine and warmth. I love holidays in France, French food, French clothes. I love Marmite and books and shopping. I also love my dog, my mother and my husband – although not necessarily in that order! We all say that we love various things – people, places, music, food, for instance. We use 'love' in many different ways, mostly to describe what we feel about people or places or things. But emotions are ephemeral and can change; some feelings of love are deep, maybe for a close family member, while other feelings of 'love' simply mean that we prefer one thing to another.

What's special about the kind of love Paul talks about? Why search for it? What difference will it make?

A special love

Real love

True love will go out of its way to do something for the one who is loved. Sheldon Vanauken and his wife, Davey, determined that because of their love they would each do whatever was asked by the other. So, they reasoned, if one of them were to ask for water in the night, for instance, the other should unhesitatingly fetch it. A mother might do that for her sick child, nurses do the same for patients in hospital. But how many of us would happily get up in the middle of the night to take a glass of water to a stranger or to someone we don't know, in order to show love?

Real, true love was demonstrated by God at Calvary, when he showed us that he loved us enough to send his only Son to die instead of us. We were 'dead through trespasses and sins . . . But God, who is rich in mercy, out of the great love with which he loved us, even when we were dead through our trespasses, made us alive together with Christ' (Ephesians 2:1, 4–5). He showed real love for us even when we were unlovable. Jesus said we are to love one another just like that – as he has loved us.

Unending love

1 Corinthians 13 must be quoted out of context more than almost any other chapter in the Bible. This beautiful eulogy about love is often read at wedding services, but it isn't specifically about romantic love at all. It is actually describing how every Christian

should be using the gifts God has given them, but with love. Without love it all means nothing. This is how God designed us to work together as his people: serving one another in love. This is the love that puts the other person first, ensures that their needs are met first, and then goes further and gives a little bit extra. This is the love that willingly fetches water in the night. Love like that is intended to be in our hearts for others – because God loves them and it's a way we can show them that love.

When we lived in Norwich, we had the privilege of working with Gordon Bridger, who was our vicar. On one occasion he was preaching about 1 Corinthians 13, and he asked whether we could each read through it and put our own name in the place of the word 'love'. It's a very humbling exercise:

'__ (your name) is patient; __ is kind; __ is not envious or boastful or arrogant or rude. __ does not insist on her own way; __ is not irritable or resentful; __ does not rejoice in wrongdoing, but rejoices in the truth. __ bears all things, believes all things, hopes all things, endures all things. Love never ends.'

Searching for love

Tessa is a medical student, and she has been working with a group of students on various projects in a training hospital. Tessa and some of the others found Judy, another member of the group, very difficult. Judy had an unpleasant attitude to the patients, was rude to everyone she met, and preferred to spend her evenings in nightclubs drinking with the men until she had to be half-carried home. Tessa tried to avoid Judy and Judy's caustic remarks about the 'God squad'.

Talking on the phone one evening to her mother, Tessa complained about Judy, expecting her mother's sympathy. To her surprise, her mother gently asked her whether she had prayed not just for Judy, but for her own attitude to be changed. Her mother promised to pray for both girls. Tessa humbly went to God to apologise for her lack of love for Judy, and asked for the Holy Spirit to change her heart and to work in her to give her a new attitude of love.

Tessa was surprised to realise, a few weeks later, that her attitude was indeed changing and that she was able to begin to love Judy. She plucked up courage to invite Judy to a special evening for students at church – and Judy accepted. After listening intently to the speaker, Judy told Tessa she had known something was missing in her life and that she had been exceptionally unhappy and longing to be different. She'd heard something that night which had begun to change her and could she come again?

Tessa's mother told me all this just earlier this week. What really struck us both was the way Tessa could see that God was honouring her prayer to have love in her heart to help someone else. As soon as Tessa confessed her lack of love and asked God to begin to change her, the love she needed was put in her heart.

We need to 'pursue' love just because it doesn't always come naturally to us. One translation says, 'Make love your aim' (1 Corinthians 14:1, RSV). It's aiming for the goal, setting the course, following the quarry. It suggests that I need to make a conscious decision to determine which course I'm on – and Paul says the goal should be love. Tessa's heart was changed when she talked with God about her attitude to Judy, and we can pray for the Holy Spirit of God to begin his work in us so that we become more loving, more like Jesus.

Showing love

Grape peeling

When I first fell in love with the man who is now my husband, I wanted to show him just how much he meant to me, and so I invited him to supper in the flat I shared with a friend. I missed all my lectures that day and spent the whole time preparing and cooking a very special meal, which included a pavlova for dessert. The first pavlova was a disaster, so I had to make a second one, which I covered with sliced bananas and grapes – and every single grape was halved, depipped and peeled! My love for him was demonstrated in the care I took over that food. As soon as someone falls in love, they want to show the beloved how much they are loved. It makes a difference to what they do and how they treat one another. I have to say I have never peeled another grape for my husband since. I don't think I have ever peeled an orange for him either, but I have one friend who always peels her husband's oranges for him as a tiny demonstration of her continuing love.

Within a loving relationship we almost expect love to be automatic, even though it often isn't. But what about in everyday life? Cathy tidies up the songbooks after the service every Sunday, Olwen sends a card to people from church who are in hospital, and Jill visits them. Meg is always baking, and will often make an extra batch to take round to welcome newcomers. Linda invites people who are alone to Sunday lunch and Tricia organises parcels of clothes and soap to send to children in Romania. Little acts of service.

Foot washing

Jesus said if we love him we will keep his commands (John 14:15), and he commanded us to love one another just as he has loved us (John 13:34) so that everyone will see that we are his disciples.

He showed how it works when he washed the disciples' feet. None of them wanted to do the job which was normally performed by the most junior slave: kneeling to wash tired, dirty, smelly feet which had tramped in open sandals through the dirt and dust. Jesus silently and graciously set the example. He tied a towel around his waist, poured a bowlful of water, and washed and dried all those feet. Then he told them that if he, their Lord and teacher, had washed their feet, then they 'also ought to wash one another's feet' (John 13:14). It takes a special kind of love to bend to do that. 'Real love begins where nothing is expected in return' (Antoine de Saint-Exupery).

This love puts the needs of others before our own needs and does whatever is necessary to serve and help, because it is true love. It gives us servant hearts as it follows the example of Jesus. Putting others first doesn't come easily to us. The current philosophy is one of self-assertiveness. 'Ten steps to asserting yourself!' 'How to have time for yourself!' 'Learn to say NO!' were just a few of the articles in the magazines I saw on the newsagents' shelf. While some of us need to learn to be more self-confident, or to say no occasionally, most of us don't have too much of a problem with thinking of ourselves first. But God gave us a specific command, 'In love serve one another' (Galatians 5:13, NIV).

Serving others

Doris is an elderly lady who remembers helping her parents in the shop they used to run. In those days there was none of the 'self-service' we are familiar with. Every customer was treated as an individual and served by the shop-keeper. Doris recalls, 'I was taught never to ask a customer, "Is that all?" but to enquire, "What else can I get for you?" so that the person knew we were willing to reach any shelf to find the required articles.' It's an attitude of 'going the second mile', doing whatever one can to help, which Doris has had throughout her life in the way she has always been ready to help others.

What would Jesus do?

Serving is a way of life rather than the odd job done to salve a conscience. It is learning to love as Jesus loved. It's the kind of love which says, 'What would Jesus do in this situation?' and 'What can I do to show the love of Jesus here?' It says, 'Whatever it takes, God,' knowing that it may be costly, in terms of our time or our energy or our money or ourselves. My American friend, MaryLou, came back from Chicago with a new embroidered bracelet. It has the initials 'WWJD' on it, and it caught her eye in a church bookshop. Christians are wearing these bracelets to remind themselves: What Would Jesus Do? Actions speak louder than words: what do our actions say about our relationship with Jesus?

Going the extra mile

In 1966, Jackie Pullinger went to the Walled City in Hong Kong, a dreadful slum area now demolished. She went to work among the drug addicts, the prostitutes and the gangsters who ruled the filthy narrow streets with brutality and extortion. She arrived with nothing except the knowledge that God was calling her to serve him by serving these people, and that he would equip her with all that she needed. Jackie was immediately plunged into the world of crime: drugs, theft, murder, and all the pain and casualties they caused. Yet the second time she entered the Walled City, she was filled with a tremendous sense of joy, which she thought was strange in such a revolting place. The sense filled her each time she was in the Walled City, and she realised that it was the sense of knowing that she was serving God and that he was leading her. She gave herself completely to working with the addicts, and helping them to understand what God had done for them in Jesus by showing them what he was like through her actions. She worked tirelessly, often going with little or no sleep in order to be available when she was needed. Jackie felt that, although Jesus had said to walk the extra mile with someone who asks you to walk one mile with them, some Christians wouldn't mind doing the one extra mile, some might even go two, but rarely would anyone go three. And the people she worked with needed a marathon.

How far are you and I prepared to go in serving others for the love of God?

Putting it into practice

• Meditate on Galatians 5:22–6:10, and ask the Spirit to be at work in your heart to produce his fruit in your life.
• I find it helpful to pray, 'Lord, give me a servant's heart, willing to be willing to do anything for you.'
• Pursue love: Colossians 3:12–15.

9

Designed to Make a Difference

You, my brothers, were called to be free. But do not use your freedom to indulge the sinful nature; rather, serve one another in love. (Galatians 5:13, NIV)

A bright red pillar box, barely a foot high, stood in front of my young son. With great determination he was trying to 'post' a blue triangle through a hole in the top, but because the hole was square, the task was impossible. He pushed and pushed, and began to get very cross and frustrated when the triangle refused to go through. The harder he tried the worse it got, and eventually he shouted and threw the triangle away in rage and disgust. He knew it was meant to fit in somehow, but he hadn't yet grasped the full implications of there being a different shaped hole for each of the coloured shapes. Initially, he tried to ram the shapes into any hole and became very cross when they refused to go in. Eventually, he learnt that certain shapes fitted certain holes, and suddenly it all worked easily!

Understanding that I am called to follow the example of Jesus and be a servant in my attitude to others means that I should be willing to do anything for God. Understanding that God made each of us unique, with our own 'shape', means that I realise I'm designed to serve in a specific way. We each have our own particular 'slot' where our shape fits in easily. Sometimes because we know we ought to be serving and making a difference for God, we have tried to ram our shape into any vacant hole, and that leads to frustration and isn't very productive. When we do the job for which we are best suited, we work efficiently, we enjoy it and we get more satisfaction from it. We are therefore able to keep on when the going gets tough, and we are productive and fulfilled.

There are little jobs which have to be done but are not necessarily anyone's 'shape'. Love helps us to do those. If most of the time we are doing things which are our 'shape-slot', we will really enjoy what we are doing. Then, because we know what we do best, we are able to help others, bring them closer to God, making a difference in their lives as well as in our own.

Discovering our shape

When do you work best and when are you most productive? What natural talents and skills do you have? What spiritual gifts has God given to you? What desires has he put on your heart? All these different areas help to define the shape God has made you and which slot he wants you to fill. We need to allow God to show us his design, to learn to see ourselves as he sees us, and to be open to new possibilities. Step outside what you've always thought or been told by others and see yourself from God's perspective. In the Old Testament, David was seen by his family as 'only' the young shepherd boy; God saw him as a man after his own heart, the leader and shepherd of his people.

Functioning well

Lynn is an English teacher. She always takes a selection of books and texts with her to a lesson, and decides what to do when she gets there depending on how the children are behaving and what would be the best thing to do that day. Alison is also an English teacher, but she has each lesson planned meticulously and knows exactly which topics will be covered when. Lynn begins the lesson when everyone has arrived; Alison starts on time, whether everyone is there or not. Both teachers love their work and get excellent results from their pupils, but they function in very different ways. When she goes away on holiday, Lynn prefers to drive until she finds somewhere pretty and then stop; Alison plans her route carefully and has her accommodation booked in advance. In the supermarket, Lynn browses and chooses things which appeal; Alison has a list of menus for the week and the ingredients she needs to make them. Lynn and Alison are total opposites in the way they function best.

Each of us has our own style and temperament and ways in which we work best. Did you find Lynn's ways appealing, or Alison's? Or are you happy with either? Read each of these descriptions, and see which best describes you.

Flexible   Spontaneous, laid-back, make it up as you go along, play it by ear, decide when you get there, see where it leads, open to possibilities, likes variety, thinks after it's done, files later or not at all.

Planned   Prioritises, makes lists and ticks as jobs are done, follows a routine, timetable, shopping is listed in order of the supermarket layout, meets deadlines, sticks to a plan, likes to know what needs to be done and when.

Introverted   Personal, private, likes solitude, hates big parties and strangers, can be withdrawn or shy.

Extroverted Outgoing, vigorous, social, goes forward to meet people, often talkative, likes action.

Relational   Prefers people and getting to know them, concerned with feelings, communication is important, likes team work.

Rational   Prefers to concentrate on the job, less worried about how it affects others, focuses on the procedure, often works alone.

Each of us has a tendency towards one or two of these areas, and that determines how we work best. Barbara is flexible and extroverted. She's spontaneous and gets on well with everyone she meets. She loves chatting to people and is an asset on the church visiting team; she's on the rota for welcoming people into church and she quickly makes them feel at home. Fiona is very planned, a little bit introverted and rational. She likes regular, ongoing things to get on with and get finished. She photocopies, folds and staples the church magazine each month, and then organises the ones which have to be posted. Moira is happy to be either flexible or planned – she's nicely in the middle, but she is rational and quite shy. So she is good at doing jobs which vary, but need to be finished quickly and don't involve her getting to know other people. She counts the collection each week, and gets the room ready for Alpha meetings.

Barbara, Fiona and Moira serve God in different ways but each of them plays an important part in the life of their church. Without any one of them there would be a 'gap'. They *could* do each other's tasks if necessary – Barbara is perfectly capable of counting the collection and would fill in if Moira was away, but she would find it very tedious. Fiona *could* smile at visitors and hand them a hymn book if Barbara was ill – although Fiona would find it hard work and wouldn't say very much to them.

We can each work in areas where we don't naturally find it easy, and we will manage; but we may not survive for very long, and may get exhausted, disillusioned or bored.

Natural talents and skills

Pippa writes glorious songs – words and music. She has an enormous electric keyboard which she uses for composing and for performing, taking it to churches and often singing in evangelistic guest services. Pippa's music is a natural talent: she has never had a music lesson in her life, and cannot read a note of music.

Julia plays the church keyboard for Sunday services. She's a competent player, but she has worked hard at it. Many years of lessons and many hours of practice have given her confidence and accuracy, and her leading inspires people as they sing and worship God. Her skill has been learnt, but she is good at it and she really enjoys playing.

What natural talents and learnt skills do you have? What do you enjoy doing, and are confident with and do well? Perhaps you too are musical; or you can paint, or garden, or dance. Perhaps you programme computers, make videos, maintain cars. Or you write poetry, throw pots, keep the books balanced.

When the Israelites were given instructions by God for building the tent of the covenant with its mercy seat and the ark of the covenant and all the beautiful furnishings, a team of craftsmen were chosen to 'devise artistic designs' (Exodus 31:4). Bezalel was chosen because he was skilful, with 'ability, intelligence, and knowledge in every kind of craft' (v3), but God then further blessed him for this job by filling him with 'divine spirit' and God gave 'skill to all the skillful' (vv 3,6). Bezalel, the man chosen for the artistic design, was specially chosen, equipped and filled with God's Spirit, to use the ability he already had for the greater glory of God. What he designed and created then helped people in their worship of God.

What are the two or three things you think of as your natural talents and your acquired skills? They are an intrinsic part of you and make you special and unique. Sometimes I look at what others can do, and I sigh, and wish I could sing like Freda, or sew like Pamela, or preach like Kim. I forget what God has already given to me. He gives to each one of us liberally. I need to own and develop what he has given to me and use it to his glory. 'Whatever you do, do everything for the glory of God' (1 Corinthians 10:31).

Spiritual gifts

Dorothy was a familiar figure at every prayer meeting at the church in Norwich where my husband was a curate. She had a real gift for prayer, particularly praying for missionaries. No matter what the prayer meeting was about, Dorothy prayed for the missionaries she knew. She also prayed for God to send out more missionaries – and if you were on her list and she prayed for you to be a missionary, watch out: God answered Dorothy's prayers. Her intercessory prayer was a gift she had been given by God, and Dorothy used it, and thereby learnt more and more about her gift and the giver. She certainly made a difference in the lives of many people.

Michelle has a gift of evangelism. She has a wonderful ability to share her faith with others and communicate the good news of Jesus. She does this quietly and effectively, talking naturally with those she meets. Michelle isn't a preacher – she doesn't stand at the front of a large stadium and proclaim to thousands at a time, but she is still an evangelist, 'gossiping' her faith to others. Not everyone she talks to becomes a Christian, although many do; but she goes on exercising her gift, learning every time, and depending totally on God each time she tells someone else about him. Lots of women are very grateful to Michelle for the difference she has made in their lives by introducing them to Jesus.

Linda always has her kettle on and is constantly making a cup of tea or coffee for whoever has dropped in to see her. She is a wonderful cook too, and most Sundays she invites someone to lunch after church. On Wednesday evenings, one of the housegroups meets in her home – she is thrilled to have others come to her home, and although she never leads a Bible study and rarely prays out loud, she always makes everyone feel welcome, and bakes melt-in-your-mouth biscuits for them. Linda has the gift of hospitality, and she welcomes and invites, and provides and cares for, those who need some TLC, a place to relax, home cooking. Her open home and her welcoming smile have helped time and time again.

It's not very British to say someone has a gift, and certainly not to say it of oneself. 'We are so very 'umble,' as Uriah Heep said. But God loves to give gifts to each of us, and he is a generous and lavish giver. 'God's gifts put man's best gifts to shame,' wrote Elizabeth Barrett Browning. And what he gives to us we are to use and give away, otherwise the flow dries up. In a sense, we are to be like drain-pipes; not a very beautiful analogy, perhaps, but a useful one. If the drain-pipe becomes blocked and the water can't escape, everything inside becomes stagnant and putrid, and fresh supplies can't run through. Unblock the pipe, and the water flows continuously. So God pours his gifts into us, and as we use them and make a difference for him, he can pour more fresh supplies in. But if we try to hang on to what we have and don't use it, then we can become stagnant and useless.

There are many different gifts, but they are all given by the same Spirit (1 Corinthians 12:4) and they are given to us so that we can care for one another (1 Corinthians 12:25). Paul writes that we are like a body, which only functions properly when each part does what it is supposed to (1 Cor 12:12,27). Peter tells us to serve one another with our gifts (1 Peter 4:10).

Have you ever read the lists of the gifts? They are in Romans 12:6–8, 1 Corinthians 12 and Ephesians 4:11–13. Some gifts are mentioned more than once. What makes your heart beat faster as you read? What do you enjoy? What do you do well? Where has God used you in the past? What do your Christian friends notice that God blesses in you? (Ask them.) Where do you want to make a difference? Keep these questions in your mind as you go through this description of the gifts.

Administration:	Involves understanding, implementing, organising, planning.
Apostleship:	Involves initiating, persisting, overseeing, pioneering.
Compassion:	Involves caring, supporting, comforting, patience and kindness.
Discernment:	Involves accurately judging, distinguishing between right and wrong.
Encouragement:	Involves affirming, motivating, encouraging, strengthening.
Evangelism:	Involves sharing and communicating the gospel effectively.
Faith:	Involves believing and trusting God confidently, praying accordingly.
Giving:	Involves giving freely, generously, unselfishly, joyfully.
Hospitality:	Involves welcoming, caring, providing, inviting.
Healing:	Involves praying humbly and confidently for restoration.
Interpretation:	Involves carefully and courageously interpreting the gift of tongues.
Knowledge:	Involves learning, studying, researching, sharing information.

Leadership:	Involves inspiring, motivating, guiding, influencing, dreaming dreams.
Miracles:	Involves faith, trust, confidence, prayer, perception, understanding.
Pastoring:	Involves guiding, caring, nurturing, supporting, overseeing.
Prophecy:	Involves conviction, boldness, proclaiming and revealing God's truth.
Serving:	Involves working, supporting, reliably meeting any needs, humility.
Teaching:	Involves explaining, communicating, understanding, enthusing.
Tongues:	Involves speaking aloud in a God-given language.
Wisdom:	Involves listening to God, explaining, carefully applying truth, advising.

No list is exclusive and the New Testament lists are not identical. But putting them together gives us a good base to begin to search for the gifts God may give to us. We are told to 'eagerly desire the greater gifts' (1 Corinthians 12:31, NIV). What picture does that image give you – perhaps a small girl longing for the chocolates to take home at the end of a party, or the dog waiting expectantly for mealtime, or the reporter who will stop at nothing to get an exclusive first report. They are eagerly desiring; do we eagerly desire gifts from God and plead in prayer for them?

What are the gifts God has given to you? Every Christian has at least one of these gifts; some have two or three. The gifts may be at different levels. For instance, leadership may be exercised by the leader of a large church of a thousand people, or by the leader of a small home fellowship group of ten. Evangelism can be a gift used in preaching to a large stadium full of tens of thousands of people, or by talking to a neighbour over coffee. Giving may be a cheque for a million pounds, or a home-baked cake. Administration might be running a large parachurch office, or organising the church cleaning rota. Any gift can be used at any level; and every gift needs to be exercised or, like a muscle, it will wither and be useless. Sometimes we will fail – the evangelist doesn't convert everyone she talks to, the leader sometimes lacks vision; but the more we use our gifts, the stronger they get.

Special desires

Sitting in a church service where the music is dull makes me frustrated; I long to get up and do something about it. I want others to know just how wonderful it can be to worship God in song, to enter into his presence and to join in the worship of heaven which never ceases. So I was thrilled when I was given the opportunity to help lead the music at our church. I'm really enthusiastic about it and it's no chore to have to go to Monday night practices or turn up early before the service in order to make last-minute checks and adjustments. Well, most of the time. There are days when I feel tired or cross – but I want to help others to worship God better and to share the same vision.

There are five clues to which shape-slot God has in mind for me:
If it's not done well I want to work on it.

I really enjoy it.

I don't find it a chore when it involves time and effort.

It seems obvious to me that it should receive top priority.

It's helpful to identify your shape-slot so that you can serve God in the right place. What has God put on your heart? Answering some of these questions might help you to clarify your thoughts:

* What do you enjoy doing?
* What would you like to change/improve/start in your church?
* What do you wish you could make other people see is so very important?
* How do you see yourself when you daydream? What do you wish you were doing?
* What would your family or your friends say you are passionate about?
* What makes you lean forward in a conversation, talking enthusiastically, longing to make me understand?

It may help to classify some areas which could be your speciality. (But don't limit yourself to these: they are just examples.)

People

- An age group: Pre-school children, or the retired, or students.

- A particular group: The housebound, the bereaved, prisoners, singles, overworked executives, children from broken homes.

- Their interests: Sport, art, theatre; their homes or gardens.

- Their origins: Different countries, ethnic groups.

Causes

- Issues in society: Racial prejudice, the environment, abortion, AIDS.

- Issues of Christ: Witnessing, interceding in prayer.

The Church

- Day-to-day running: Cleaning, typing, gardening, tidying, washing up.

- Services: Welcoming, music, flowers, coffee, banners.

- Special events: Organising, catering, decorating, officiating.

Perhaps you can already see one or more areas where you long to help others and work for God. If that isn't clear yet, take time to pray about the different areas. Think about it when you are in church, or at your mid-week small group, or with other Christians. Ask people who know you well what they think you are really interested in. Then you might like to come back and read through this section again.

Time out

There are times in our lives when we're not able to make the difference we really want to. There can be very good reasons for this: a new baby, moving house, a big project at work, illness. Although these are usually temporary, they can become excuses for long-term avoidance.

Circumstances

Diane used to work long hours which involved travelling, but which provided a huge paycheck at the end of each month. The hours took their toll and she was exhausted. She also knew that spiritually she was struggling – she hadn't the time or the energy to spare for the things of God. By the time she got home from work and had a meal it was too late to go to home group. On Sundays she slept in late to catch up on some rest, and often had to do odd things around the house which had been ignored during the week, and by the evening she was mentally gearing up for Monday morning again. She was drifting away from God and from his people.

Diane loved her job as a barrister, and she was good at it, but gradually she realised that other things were as important to her, and that God was far more important. She took a long, hard look at her life and decided that such an enormous salary wasn't actually necessary: she needed only sufficient to pay the expenses, not to store up treasure on earth. No, Diane didn't give it all up, but she did re-evaluate her lifestyle and made some radical changes. She 'downshifted', worked shorter hours and moved to a small home, which meant her bills decreased.

Diane volunteered to use her skills and her gifts of discernment and compassion to aid some in the church who needed legal and financial advice. She does a few hours only occasionally, but it has made a difference to many people. Diane has time for God in her life again, and he has given her a whole new meaning to life. She has found her shape-slot.

Spiritual maturity

We are all at different stages in our Christian lives. We all begin with new birth and need spiritual milk (1 Peter 2:2) but we should then go on to grow in our relationship with Jesus. As we mature in our Christian lives, we can be used by God as we learn to be more open to his leading and his guiding.

Alice became a Christian on an Alpha course. She is a young mother with three children, and she has a husband who works long hours. Becoming a Christian was a revolutionary idea to the whole family, but Alice had met Jesus, and she knew that her life would never be the same again. Having had no Christian teaching before, Alice began at the very beginning and was soon reading the Bible, both by herself and with a small group of others. She discovered the joy of knowing that God was pouring his gifts on her. She was enthusiastic and she had the gift of evangelism. She was telling all her friends what had happened in her life, and the difference Jesus can make. Some wanted to know more, or to become Christians themselves, but Alice didn't know how to help them to do that. She was still too young a Christian herself to be much more help, and so she wasn't able to use her gift to its full extent. But she took her friends to other Christians who did know what to say and do, and in watching them, Alice learnt and understood more and more. Now, several years later, Alice is even more effective in her witness and is a bold evangelist for God. She is making a difference in the lives of many women as she tells them about God. Her gift has matured along with her walk with God.

Sin

If there is disobedience or lack of repentance, broken relationships or bad attitudes in our lives, we will not be able to make a difference for God. 'Let us also lay aside every weight and the sin that clings so closely, and let us run with perseverance the race that is set before us, looking to Jesus, the pioneer and perfecter of our faith . . . Consider him . . . so that you may not grow weary or lose heart' (Hebrews 12:1–3).

Making a difference

It is very exciting to discover what shape God intended us to be and to realise that there is a slot which is just the right shape for us to fill. Perhaps you feel your slot is to help with something which is already happening in your church family. You will be able to join in and make your contribution. Find out who is in charge of that area and volunteer your help. Or maybe your interest is a new area, and you are excited about the possibilities opening up. Find two or three others who have the same 'shape' as you do, and start praying together about the new venture, asking for tremendous wisdom, help and tact as you introduce the idea to your church minister or leader. These are exciting times God has called us to live in and there is great potential to do wonderful things with him and for him.

Achieving something worthwhile can often be demanding and costly. But if it's something we really want to do, we persevere, determined to achieve our aim. The results can make us exuberant, that wonderful feeling of hard work which has led to an effective and worthwhile conclusion. There was tremendous joy on the face of my small child as he discovered just how to get the different shapes into the pillarbox shape-sorter, and he had great fun doing it himself and showing others how to do it too. Once we have each discovered our own shape and fitted it into our own shaped slot, there will be joy, fun and excitement. There will also be the hard times when things seem to go wrong or we don't seem to be getting anywhere. But knowing that we are in the place God designed us for will help us to keep going in his strength, and encourage one another to keep going too.

We may not always see the results in this life, but one day the Father will be able to say, 'Well done, thou good and faithful servant' (Matthew 25:21, KJV). Knowing that we have made a difference for eternity is certainly worth while, don't you think?

Putting it into practice

• Read 1 Corinthians 12, asking God to speak to you. How can you begin to play a part within the 'body' (the Church)?
• Four main areas in this chapter help define what makes you your unique 'shape'. You might like to work out your own 'shape' and record it in your journal:

    temperament/style
    natural talents/skills
    spiritual gifts
    special desires.

- Where and how might you make a difference for God?

10

Designed to Build for the Future

For surely I know the plans I have for you, says the Lord, plans for your welfare and not for harm, to give you a future with hope. (Jeremiah 29:11)

I stood gazing into the window of an antique jewellery shop in Bath. In the centre of the display was a ring which made my heart stop. This was it – a beautiful old diamond solitaire I would choose for my engagement ring.

It was time to meet Kim. Excitedly, I suggested we go together to look at the ring. We knew we were to be married eventually, even though he hadn't formally proposed. Although we couldn't be married for eighteen months, and didn't want a long engagement, we decided to buy the ring. Or, at least, I bought the ring as I was working and he was an impoverished student! We agreed that he would keep the ring until we became 'officially' engaged. It would be our secret.

We returned to his parents' home, and they guessed almost immediately that something had happened. Our happiness could not be contained. We burst out with the news of our plans for the future. We couldn't keep it to ourselves!

The exciting plans God has for us are far too good to be kept to ourselves. Once we discover that he's designed, chosen and called us, that he wants a deep relationship with us and bestows grace and forgiveness on us, that we can make a lasting difference by serving him, then we will be bursting to tell others! It will be difficult to keep it to ourselves sometimes. We'll be able to encourage other women in their spiritual journey, helping them to grow.

Built to lead

Maybe that's a daunting thought. Many of us don't think of ourselves as leaders. We imagine that all leaders are important people who are influential on a large scale, but a leader can also be someone who is in front of one or two people, *showing* them the way. And actions speak louder than words. A woman who actively demonstrates that her priority is to become the person God intends is naturally someone others want to be with, to learn from and to imitate. What we *are* speaks much louder than what we *say*. Our lives can point others towards God's design for them – and knowing that we are living examples to others does help to keep us up to the mark as well.

Maybe we don't feel capable, or committed, or confident, not like leaders. Fortunately we don't have to do it in our own strength. 'Not that we are competent of ourselves to claim anything as coming from us; our competence is from God, who has made us competent' (2 Corinthians 3:5). It's the unflattering but useful drain-pipe analogy again, as we allow God to use us and to flow through us and out to others. It's Jesus in us that is attractive to others; it's the Holy Spirit at work in us that enables us to lead others, to 'provoke one another to love and good deeds' (Hebrews 10:24). God has equipped us with everything we need, and we can be confident in his provision.

Model

I told my children several times how to work the washing machine. 'It's easy – pop the clothes in, add a soap-ball of powder, and switch it on.' But they still shied away from using it, saying they were frightened they might break it, spoil the clothes or cause a flood. Feeble excuses. Until one day I took them to the machine and showed them exactly how to do a load of washing – how to sort the clothes, how much powder to use, where to put the conditioner, which programme to use. Once I had demonstrated how to do it, and stood beside them while they did it for themselves, there was no excuse. They could copy what I had done and were confident and able to use the machine too.

'Be imitators of me, as I am of Christ,' Paul wrote. (1 Corinthians 11:1) The most powerful message, and the most effective, is to *show* others. Older women are instructed to teach the younger women (Titus 2:3–4), and the original Greek word translated 'teach' implies demonstrating, showing, not just speaking.

Susannah had eighteen children, and regarded them as the mission-field to which God had called her. Susannah faithfully prayed for her children. When she threw her voluminous apron over her head, the children knew that mother was not to be disturbed because she was talking with God. 'There are two things to do with the gospel,' she said. 'Believe it and behave it.' Because she behaved it, and modelled what she believed, her sons followed her example. Bible study, fasting and praying were habits caught from their mother. In turn, her sons John and Charles Wesley were influential too. John became a famous open-air itinerant preacher. Many thousands believed as the Holy Spirit poured out times of refreshing and revival. Charles was a poet. He wrote over 6,500 hymns, many of which we still sing today: 'Love divine, all loves excelling', 'Jesus Christ is risen today', 'Hark! the herald angels sing', 'And can it be'.

Enthuse

Every time I meet Jan she tells me about the latest book she's read. She enthuses about the author, the plot, the context, the style, and by the time she's finished, I want to read the book too.

Being enthusiastic is infectious and if we are on fire for God, others will catch alight too. God is at work and it encourages us to talk with our friends about it. Constantly tell his story, constantly tell your story, John Wimber used to urge people. Tell others what God is doing in your life and the difference it makes to you and others will begin to be infected by your enthusiasm.

Liz sends beautiful cards with a few words of encouragement. Once a week Stephanie spends her lunch hour praying with a friend going through a difficult time. Mary, at home with a young family, is the first telephone link in a prayer chain and is always very understanding. Think about what you have to share with others. Has God taught you something recently? Pass it on to someone else. Has a friend prayed for you when you had a difficult time? Do the same for another friend. Have you felt the extraordinary love of God? Maybe someone else needs to be reminded of God's love. Be creative in thinking of ways to enthuse others. You can share what you know, and you can share what you have, but the best is to share yourself. As you do, God blesses you through it too.

Shepherd

One Sunday morning after church, I was approached by a young woman whom I knew only a little. Rather diffidently, she asked if I would 'shepherd' her: spend a short time regularly to meet together, pray and read the Bible, and for me to teach her more about God. I was stunned! At a low point in my own spiritual life, I had little to offer, and shrank from having that exposed. Yet I was the rector's wife, and had to agree. 'Lord, use me if you can!' was my desperate cry. I didn't feel like doing this, felt totally useless, but I was willing for God to work and use me. Over the next three years, Wendy and I met regularly – and I've already told you a little of what happened as we studied God's word, prayed for one another, shared openly and honestly, laughed and cried together.

I was also passing on what I had received. Eleanor spent time with me when I was at university. She took me on houseparties to train me to lead; she prayed; she lent me Christian books (including those of Amy Carmichael). Even now, she occasionally shepherds me, praying with me and talking things through. Wendy has been a leader in the youth group, and shepherded Sarah. Sarah is now shepherding younger teenage girls. It's exciting to see God using women in this way.

Jesus chose his closest followers carefully, after praying. From the twelve, he chose just three to be more intimate with him. As we follow his example, we will prayerfully choose a tiny number to encourage and shepherd. The investment of our time and effort is immensely rewarding as we see others develop. Our own devotion grows at the same time.

Build to last

'Be careful then how you live, not as unwise people but as wise, making the most of the time' (Ephesians 5:15–16). What are we building our lives around? Will I influence others – or do I care more about money, power, fame? Am I wanting to build the kingdom of God, to give my life for something that will last for ever? Do I 'delight' to do his will (Psalm 1:2)?

'If I perish, I perish!'

God chooses to work through individuals who are obedient to him no matter what the cost. Esther was prepared to do what was needed to save God's people from the wrath of King Ahasuerus and his official, Haman. She had been made queen through unusual circumstances. The previous queen, Vashti, had refused to obey the king's summons, and the public demonstration of self-assurance and rebelliousness was such a bad example to everyone else, that she was deposed (Esther 1:17–19). A new queen had to be found, and all the most beautiful young women were prepared. The king chose Esther, who did not reveal that she was of Jewish descent.

Later, when the Jews were under threat of annihilation, Esther's uncle, Mordecai, instructed her to plead the cause of her people. For Esther to enter the king's presence without being sent for was against the law. She could be put to death for such an action. Yet her uncle told her that perhaps she had been made queen 'for just such a time as this' (Esther 4:14). God is not mentioned by name, but the implication is clear. This is God's plan to rescue his people. Esther was willing to be used by God: 'If I perish, I perish' (Esther 4:16). She didn't trust in her beauty or her position but in God. She, her maids and Mordecai all fasted and prayed for three days before taking any action. Then, Esther was ready.

Esther's faith saved her people. Their enemy, Haman, was overturned and Mordecai elevated in rank (Esther 10:3). He was then able to uphold his people and intercede for them with the king.

Esther was obedient to God. She didn't hesitate; she chose to be used by God. It doesn't matter who you are, what your position is or what gifts you have. If you choose to be submissive to God he will fill you with the power of his Spirit and use you. He may not use you to free a nation (although he might), and he may not make you a queen (though he could), but he will use you to be influential for him, to encourage others and to enable them to grow in their spiritual lives too. 'Encourage each other every day . . . Let us do all that we can to help one another's faith' (Hebrews 3:13; 10:25, JB Phillips).

Priorities

I've made a will and I've decided what I want to happen to my most precious belongings when I come to the end of my physical life. It's to help my family sort things out. But it's not much good to me – I shall be going on to other things. It's not much use having huge amounts of money or jewellery to leave behind (I haven't). All that matters is what I've built to last for eternity. Somehow a will seems rather unimportant when faced with eternity. What will be important to me then? How does that affect my priorities now?

Eleanor says she's going to heaven and she wants to take as many others with her as possible. That defines her priorities. If we define what's important, we can live by our priorities and not by the pressures which easily take over.

My priorities:

1. God: To be open to God's plans for my life. To learn to be more like Jesus. To let the Holy Spirit change me.
2. My family, who are entrusted to me by God.
3. My church and my friends.

Can you define your priorities?

Pyrogenic

The bonfire sent flames leaping into the air, and the heat singed leaves on the trees some distance away. It was an intense fire, but it didn't last. Eventually it died down – and our neighbours breathed sighs of relief. It gradually lost heat and as it wasn't fed it became ineffective and lukewarm.

Lukewarmness isn't demanding, it won't be challenging and it won't be exciting. But it's very easy to slip into. Pamukkale is a little town in Turkey – its name means 'cotton castle' and refers to the water deposits left on the rock face. They give the impression of a castellated building cascading down the cliff. The water in Pamukkale, certainly in older times, was not suitable for drinking. Higher up the valley, the water gushed out at Hierapolis in hot springs, wonderfully therapeutic for bathing. Further down, the water was cold and refreshing. But where the two sources met, at Pamukkale, the water became lukewarm, undrinkable, bad for the eyes, not good for anything.

Pammukale used to be called Laodicea. The early church there slipped into lukewarmness. It was 'neither hot nor cold,' so God said, 'I am about to spit you out of my mouth' (Revelation 3:16). The indictment is harsh, but the church there had to be jolted out of lukewarmness, which is no good to God. They thought they were rich and prosperous, doing quite nicely, but their priorities were misplaced. God said they were 'wretched, pitiable, poor, blind and naked', and they needed to come back to the Lord who would provide them with his gold, his clothes, his eye ointment. He was standing at the door, just waiting for the Christians to invite him back. 'Be earnest . . . to the one who conquers I will give a place with me on my throne' (Revelation 3:18–21). Lukewarmness was useless. Be hot or cold, but not lukewarm and unexciting.

Pyrogenic leaders, ignited for God, are effective. A small spark can start a large forest fire; who knows what flames God might bring from the small spark which is you? He needs us to be willing: 'If I perish, I perish.' He needs us to be living with eternity in view: prioritise. He needs us to be effective: passionately alight.

The reward Jesus offered to the Laodiceans was a place with him on his throne. Can you believe it? Jesus is offering us a place on his throne for eternity. That is his final design for your future. Will you choose to be a woman of God's design?

Putting it into practice

• Think about several people who you admire and whose walk with God is challenging to you. Ask God to show you who to ask to shepherd you. Phone her and make a date to see her. What will you ask her to teach you, share with you, pray for you?

• Make a list of several 'younger women' whom God could ask you to shepherd. Prayerfully choose one or two for investing your time, prayer and encouragement. If there are areas where you feel inadequate to do this, what steps might you take to get more training?

> Now to him who is able to keep you from falling and to present you before his glory without fault and with unspeakable joy, to the only God, our saviour, be glory and majesty, power and authority, through Jesus Christ our Lord, before time was, now, and in all ages to come, amen. (Jude: 24–25, JB Phillips)